The Ferry Boat

Finding a Credible God.

First published in Great Britain by Cadno Books in 2011

cadnobooks@btinternet.com

Michael Tod has asserted his right to be
identified as the author of this book.

www.michaeltod.co.uk

michaeltod@btinternet.com

Cover illustration by Mick Loates

www.mickloates.co.uk

Photo of author by Alan John

ISBN 9781898225072

The Ferry Boat.

Finding a Credible God.

Michael Tod

Other books by Michael Tod.

The Silver Tide

The Second Wave

The Golden Flight

Now available as a single volume

The Dorset Squirrels

Dolphin Song

God's Elephants

A Curlew's Cry (Poetry)

About the Author.

Michael Tod has written five books of fiction and one of poetry. *The Ferry Boat – Finding a Credible God* is his first non-fiction work. He came to writing at the age of 55 after a life into which he has packed many adventures, much travel and a variety of jobs.

He has always been a seeker after truth although not always aware that this was so. Reading his novels in the order in which they were written, one can follow his enlightenment. In his three squirrel books, *The Silver Tide, The Second Wave* and *The Golden Flight*, we follow a community of peace-loving Red Squirrels trying to come to terms with their country being taken over by aggressive, territory-grabbing Greys but all the time we are subtly aware of the underlying benevolent philosophy of the Reds and how they try to influence the Greys for the good of both communities. The perceptive reader will recognise parallels with both old-fashioned colonialism and modern society.

In *Dolphin Song* he builds on his life-altering experience of swimming with a wild dolphin to create an underwater world, mixing deep human emotions with the love and trauma experienced by captive dolphins yearning to be free.

In *God's Elephants* he leads us into a world of gentle elephants who rely on the help of their god, Mana, to survive in a shrinking habitat. Central to the story are the love-impregnated tusks of Tembo Jay who sacrificed himself two thousand years ago whilst teaching how other elephants can live a life of love and harmony.

Whilst creating these characters, Michael Tod became aware that he was being inspired to learn much about the real meaning of life and he has developed these ideas and themes into this book, *The Ferry Boat – Finding a Credible God.*

Contents.

The Ferry Boat

Part One

Part One. Chapter One

From Birth to Disbelief.

When I was in my mid-sixties, I discovered a god in whom I could believe.

For most of my life I considered myself to be an atheist. All the various gods 'on offer' did not satisfy two simple tests, even though I felt deep down that somehow, somewhere, there did exist something 'spiritual' – but what that spiritual *something* was, I could not describe or identify.

Until then I had had not been consciously or actively seeking a credible god; my life was just too full. I have had wonderful *up* times – earning my Queen's Scout award, joining 10,000 other boy scouts from across the world at the jamboree held near Niagara Falls when I was 18, learning the ancient craft of book-binding, marrying the best girl in town, becoming a father, grandfather and, just lately, a great-grandfather.

I have watched the sun rise from the summit of Kilimanjaro, swum with wild dolphins in Wales, Ireland and the Azores, walked through the African bush hand-in-trunk with a fully grown elephant, been kayaking with orca in Canada, enjoyed skinny-dipping in a hot spring in New Zealand, lived near a San Bushman family in Botswana and savoured the unique thrill of having my first novel published.

There have also been many *down* times – failing to win the promotions at work that I believed were my due, having to sell my house to pay bills incurred in an unsuccessful business venture and losing the next house after falling for a massive con trick. Then, more recently, collapsing mentally and physically due to stress and overwork in a futile attempt to avoid bankruptcy.

When Winston Churchill became Prime Minister in 1940, he said that he felt his whole life up until then had been preparing him for that role at that crucial time. I feel now that my whole life, both the *ups* and the *downs*, has been preparing me to help other people by sharing my discovery of a *credible* god – hence this book.

No book ever written will be universally popular. If you are a totally committed Christian with a rock-solid faith in all you have been taught, then you will almost certainly disagree with many of my conclusions but I would ask you to read on for I promise that no one holds a higher opinion of the teachings of Jesus of Nazareth than I do. If you are of any other faith, and are so convinced that what you have been taught is absolutely true and there can be no other interpretation of the nature of God, then you should probably stop reading now. If you have been persuaded by Richard Dawkins and his like that Neo-Darwinism has all the right answers (as I once was) and are as fixed in your beliefs as he appears to be, then you too would be wasting your time reading any further.

However, if you have no firm belief in a God, or find that much of the dogma associated with established religions irks you, then there might be much in the following pages to interest and excite you.

I realise now that I had been a 'seeker of truth' all my life. The Persian poet and philosopher, Omar Khayyam (1048 – 1131 A.D.) was also a Seeker and his findings are beautifully interpreted in *The Rubaiyat of Omar Khayyam*. Unfortunately he did not find what he hoped for –

Myself when young did eagerly frequent
Doctor and Saint, and heard great argument
About it and about: but evermore
Came out by that same door as in I went.

Omar's doctors and saints would have been the teachers, philosophers and holy men of his time. Four verses later he laments –

There was a Door to which I had no Key
There was a Veil through which I might not see...

Looking back I can identify with these last two lines exactly. Sadly, he failed to find the Key, nor was he able to see through the Veil and ended up finding solace in drink.

Have I been able to find Omar's missing Key and see through his all-concealing Veil? Whenever I am faced with a difficult problem, or a challenge where there may be several *right* ways to solve it, I try and stand as far back as I can so that I can see a bigger picture. In seeking a god in which I could believe, I had to stand a long, long way back. My biggest problem was that my upbringing had left me with a deep respect, even fear, of **God** and this constantly reared its head and prevented logical thought. Only when I was able to use a different name – Mana – in place of the word 'God' was I able to break through this barrier and open my mind to truly different ideas. I commend this trick to you if you have a similar problem.

In this book I will write 'God/Mana' when appropriate – read just the word that helps you most.

Looking back over recorded time, some notable figures have openly declared that *they* had the Truth about God direct from God himself; these include Moses, Jesus, Mohammed, and more recently, Joseph Smith (The founder of the Mormon faith) and Neale Donald Walsch (who wrote the *Conversations with God* books). I am sure there have been many others.

Until fairly recently anyone who was prepared to admit to 'hearing voices' was regarded as mad or even dangerous. I do believe that God has spoken to me at least twice in my life and I describe these events in detail in this book, but I do not claim to have been told 'The Whole Truth'. What I have done is link all my experiences together, given these a lot of thought and come up with what I feel is a credible answer to who, what and where God is.

[Christians and others have traditionally used the pronouns *he, him* and *his* when referring to their God, often with a capital letter – *He, Him* and *His*. This has been taken by feminists to imply that God is male and they often use *she, her* and *hers* instead. It seems obvious to me that any god is neither male nor female in the human sense but the pronouns *it* and *its* just feel wrong. I shall therefore use the traditional he, him and his and will generally use a lower case *g* when it is 'a god' and an upper case *G* when it refers to 'the God'.]

I had a wonderful childhood. From my birth until I was ten years old I lived on the south coast of England near Weymouth, a holiday resort in Dorset. Even though the

Second World War had started when I was two and much of the nearby shore and countryside was mined and cordoned off, by the time I was six and watched the preparations for D-Day, my eldest brother and I were able to swim in and sail on the Fleet Lagoon only a mile away from where we were living. Then, on my eleventh birthday, in August 1948, my family moved to South Wales to farm on the slopes of the Sugar Loaf Mountain near Abergavenny in Monmouthshire. What child could ask for more? Years of sea-oriented freedom, followed by an adolescence spent roaming the hills and valleys of the Black Mountains.

My parents were 'Church of England' – C. of E. in the shorthand of the time. When we lived in Dorset they occasionally went to the local church a short distance from our house in the sprawling village of Wyke Regis, and took with them, me and as many of my brothers and sisters as wanted to go. I remember especially the Harvest Festivals and Christmas services in the light and airy Church of All Saints on the sunny hillside above the village centre.

From the age of four, I went to a local Roman Catholic primary school run by nuns, who I recall as kindly and gentle but very strict. Naturally, we children were expected to attend prayers in the school chapel and were taught many of the Bible stories told with the sincerity of absolute confidence in their being true. My very first day was spent making a model of an oasis in a tray with sand, Plasticine palm trees and camels and with a mirror for the water. I still have a childhood memory that this was the type of landscape where Jesus lived. There was no reason for me to go to a Catholic school other than that was where the children of better-off families went.

My father was the son of a clergyman and was the J. in W. & J. Tod Ltd. – Boatbuilders – who were, after Whitehead's Torpedo Works, the largest employer in the village. My mother came from a wealthy family farming near Sherborne on the Dorset/Somerset border. She had met my father when she visited the village where my grandfather was the vicar, to teach country dancing to local girls in the early 1930s. Her parents were not happy about her marrying this impecunious but clever young man with a passion for building boats.

I was the second boy in the family, followed by two sisters and two more brothers. Such was my mother's love of children that we had two of my cousins living with us for much of the time and another teenage girl shared our holidays, as she had no brothers or sisters of her own. In addition to this, my mother ran a Girl Guide company through the latter part of the war and a Cub-Scout pack until we moved to Wales. My father was skipper of the local Sea Scouts during the same period.

I was naturally one of my mother's cub-scouts and grew up with Kipling's *Jungle Book* tales setting my moral framework as much as the earnest teachings of the nuns at school. I found the latter much harder to accept. I must have been a precocious brat because I have a clear memory of arguing with one of the nuns at school when I was about nine. She had made a comment based on a passage in the New Testament. The dialogue went something like this.

Sister Mary Catherine, 'Jesus walked across the water to where the disciples were in their boat.'

Me, putting up my hand, 'Please, Sister. You *can't* walk across water – you just sink!'

S.M.C. (kindly) '*You* can't walk on water, Michael, but Jesus could. It was a miracle - and he could perform miracles.'

Me. 'How do you know miracles were true?'

S.M.C. (patiently) 'They're all in the Gospel'.

Me. 'How do you know the Gospel's true?'

S.M.C. (less patiently) 'The Gospel *is* true. People say, "It's Gospel Truth" when something is absolutely true.'

Me. 'That doesn't mean it's true, just because people say it is. They could be lying!'

S.M.C. (severely). 'Thank you, Michael. That's enough. You must have Faith! Please be quiet now.'

No one had ever explained to me what 'Faith' was. I would define it now as 'believing in the unbelievable'.

This sort of exchange left me totally unsatisfied and now I think it was this that led me to challenge everything teachers were trying to tell me. However, the belief in a God who lived in some mysterious place called Heaven and who had a son called Jesus was never challenged. That was accepted as fact – everybody I knew believed that. God was *all-mighty* – he could do anything. He knew everything I did and everything I thought; if I did the right things I would go to Heaven when I died and, if I did bad things, I would burn in hell for ever and ever! It is a comfort to know that fewer children in this country today, are subjected to this horrific propaganda than was the case then.

It was also accepted that God was bigger than the whole Universe and had made it all in just seven days. I was taught to bow my head when I said the name 'Jesus' and to fear God as someone who would, at some time in the future, judge everything I had done and punish me accordingly. I don't recall much about God loving me – it was probably there but was overshadowed by my fear of what would happen to me because of my frequent childish misdemeanours. Even so, the concept was fixed, the rules clear and if my parents didn't openly challenge it, that was how it had to be.

In 1948 my father sold his share of the boat-works and, on my eleventh birthday, the whole family moved to a 70 acre hill farm in Wales. I started at the local Grammar School where I idled away most of the next five years but became a very keen boy scout in a troop which my mother started in the local village of Llanwenarth Citra. Actually it started as a Girl Guide company and expanded to include boys as there were not enough boys or girls to have separate meetings for each.

At first the scouts and guides met in a semi-derelict barn half a mile from our house and it was whilst walking back from there one frosty night when I was thirteen that I had a mind-blowing revelation. I looked up at the vast numbers of stars and realised that a God bigger than that could not possibly be interested in me – a tiny speck of animation on a minor planet circling a second class star on the fringe of just one of many huge galaxies. It hit me like a hammer blow and all my previous beliefs vanished overnight.

In the days that followed, I wrestled with the realisation of my own insignificance but spoke to no one else about it. My respected aunt and uncle (he was an eye surgeon) attended church every Sunday – my uncle even played the organ there – so they must believe. My mother read short prayers at the scout meetings – so she must believe. Our R.E. teacher at school, Mrs Jones, who was special to me, must believe – so who was I to have doubts? I put it all to the back of my mind and went along with the religious rituals when I was called on to do so. Besides which life was getting exciting – I was discovering girls!

When I was sixteen I met my future wife, who was then fourteen and lived in the town of Abergavenny about three miles away from the farm. Her parents were not keen on our relationship – her step-father was a teacher and naturally disapproved of my casual attitude to school work and examinations so, to gain extra opportunities to meet, we attended confirmation classes together at our local church. Frankly, what the vicar was asking us to learn, and confirm that we believed, was mostly gobbledygook to me and I just went through the motions. I could not make out the supposed relationship between eating a rice-paper wafer, taking a sip of wine from a silver mug and communing with a god, whether I believed in him or not. The subsequent confirmation service and the 'laying on of hands' by the bishop was no more than a pantomime to me, although I would not have dared to say so at the time, partly through fear of social ostracism and partly though a lingering if irrational fear of being struck down by a thunderbolt from a vengeful God (even if I did not believe in him),

Life now speeded up. I left school, knocked around on the farm for a while wondering what to do, before becoming an apprentice bookbinder and after two more years I was called up for National Service in the Royal Air Force.

Part One. Chapter Two

RAF to MLM.

Soon after joining the R.A.F., I married my childhood sweetheart even though I was not quite twenty years old. Eleven months later our first baby, a bonny girl, was born, to be followed twelve months later by a bouncing boy. I was severely criticised by my in-laws for gross irresponsibility but I have never regretted starting my family so soon. Four years later, soon after becoming a civilian again, we had another baby girl, a darling 'Lammas Lamb'.

I served in the Royal Air Force for six years, leaving when I had a crisis of conscience at the time of the Cuba confrontation. My job at that time involved guarding nuclear bombers at a base in East Anglia and I found that I could not do a job that might play even a small part in the deaths of millions of Russians (our planned targets). There were other reasons for my ending my R.A.F. service but Cuba was the catalyst.

I did learn a lot during those six years, during which I served in the U.K. and in Kenya, which was then still a British colony. Here I was accompanied by my wife and my children and it was a pleasant time for us all. Whilst in East Africa I climbed Kilimanjaro with four other airmen and, on another occasion, to the third highest point on the incredibly beautiful Mount Kenya.

The Royal Air Force taught me to give and to obey orders, how to 'rub along' with other men from wildly differing backgrounds and, during desert exercises that went wrong, I learned (painfully) how to

> *...force your heart and nerve and sinew*
> *To serve your turn long after they have gone,*
> *And so hold on when there is nothing in you*
> *Except the Will which says to them, 'Hold on'.*

(Rudyard Kipling – IF.)

While we were abroad, my mother had developed breast cancer from which she died within a year of our return, when aged just 52. It seemed most unfair both to her and to her very young grandchildren, that this so-loving woman should be taken just when she was about to contribute such a lot to their lives and to enjoy their company as they grew up.

Her early death convinced me even more that there could not be a god, especially a loving one, when such things could happen. Surely a real loving and all mighty God could organise things more fairly?

So I now had the two most powerful arguments against God's existence ranged alongside each other. Any God that might exist and was bigger than the Universe, was too remote to care about we humans far away on Earth and, even if he did, he could not be almighty and loving (as I had been taught) to allow such unfair things to happen! This confirmed my belief that God could not, and did not, exist.

However, I am quite ready to admit that thoughts of the whys and wherefores of a god were not uppermost in my mind. With three children and a mortgage, I had to put my major efforts into earning a living. I had several jobs after leaving the R.A.F. During a nine-year spell at a local manufacturing company, I progressed from Assistant Material Scheduling Clerk to Production Control Supervisor, leaving when another person was appointed to the managerial position I had expected to be mine.

It turned out to be a good move. I joined Rank Xerox, who were then the UK's leading supplier of photocopiers, at the time of their greatest success. Like most Brits I had a contempt for salesmen who were considered by most to just be 'in it for the money' and would happily rip-off customers if it increased their commission.

Rank Xerox taught me to sell ethically and put the interests of the customers as my top priority and I was with them for five enjoyable and relatively affluent years but the company had underestimated the ever-increasing Japanese competition (it was 1975) and started to seriously lose business to them.

I was tempted away to join a rival company but it didn't work out and I then joined a business selling the first of the small computers. I don't think that young people believe me when I say that I was selling a computer with a tiny 8K processor and a slow dot-matrix printer for £8,000. I *know* they don't believe me when I say that we could run an integrated accounts program fast with just 8K!

A few years later I found that developments in computer technology were advancing so quickly that it was hard to keep on top of what was happening. At the time I used to say, 'One has to read for eight hours a day to learn what had happened in the last twenty-four hours.' It meant that, whatever hardware or software one was selling, it was already out of date. Unhappy to be promoting what I knew was obsolete I therefore left the world of computers and got a job designing and selling top-of-the-range timber and glass conservatories.

My fortunes during this period were very up and down. The children were now in their teens and sometimes cash was short. A significant event occurred in the 1980s. I was in one of my least affluent periods and my wife and I needed a holiday. Seeing a fortnight in Malta advertised at a very low rate (it was January) I booked a self-catering apartment for us. I was determined that I would not listen to a radio nor read a newspaper during the whole time I was there but, on about the twelfth day, I succumbed to the temptation of a three-day-old Saturday edition of The Daily Telegraph. Sitting in the sun on the hotel balcony I read it right through, even to the last page of the weekend supplement, which I usually threw in the bin unread. This particular edition had a full-page advertisement on the back. It was headed, 'Are You Too Busy Earning a Living to Make Any Real Money?'

I read this with growing interest, as I believed then that Making Real Money was all-important. The advertisement was for a book 'that would show me how to change my life for the better' by using a simple technique but not giving a clue as to what that technique was. At £10 it seemed a good deal and, when I got home I sent off my cheque.

The book, when it arrived, told me how the author, a money-focused American, had made a fortune for himself by using a technique he called 'targeting'. His secret was to decide exactly what it was that you wanted for yourself (The Target) and set a time (which had to be reasonable) in which to achieve this. You then had to concentrate on this target many times a day and, for some reason he did not explain, picture yourself enjoying whatever it was you had chosen. He then assured you that it would turn up. Needless to say, I did not believe that it could be as simple as that but he gave an example of how he had targeted a 'Black Ford Thunderbird Car'. In an unbelievably short time and, through an impossible-to-foresee route, he became the owner of just such a vehicle. He then went on to tell how he had targeted 'A boat like the one owned by his friend, Bob' and 'A house on the coast', both of which also turned up soon after. He went on using this technique and was now a very wealthy man.

I was still sceptical but thought that I had nothing to lose by giving it a try. At that time I was driving a clapped-out Ford Zodiac which was costing quite a lot of money in repairs to keep it going. Rather half-heartedly I targeted a 'Volvo estate car' though I knew I could not possibly afford one of those. Two days later I was driving along a road I did not normally use and passed a garage with a number of used cars on the forecourt. I noticed that one of these was a Volvo estate car. Something went click in my head and I reversed back to have another look. There were in fact two Volvo estate cars each priced at about £2500 – which was far more than I could afford. Despite this, I got out of my car and walked across to look at them. An eager salesman spotted me and offered a test drive. I replied that 'I did not have £2500 to spend on a car' and he said, 'No problem, we can do hire purchase.' I countered by saying my credit status (at that time) would rule this out and he said that he 'could get round that'. The deposit would be 'Only £500 – with a monthly payment of just £50'. I laughed and said 'Where would *I* get £500?'

'I'll allow £500 part-exchange on your Ford,' he replied.

I knew that it was costing me at least £50 a month to keep the Ford on the road and, within half an hour, I had signed a deal (at an APR of 49.5%!) and drove away in a Volvo estate car – just like the one I targeted!

I still didn't believe that this had happened through targeting and that it was all due to my having 'Volvo estate car' on my mind that day.

Somewhere about this time I was recommended to read Richard Dawkins' book, *The Selfish Gene*, which influenced me hugely. Here was a logical, if bleak, explanation of how life formed and evolved on this planet. Here was an answer to the mysteries that had puzzled me for so long and I was literally trembling with suppressed excitement as I read it. There was no place in Dawkins' world for a god nor any aspect of spirituality. Neo-Darwinism explained everything! I was even more convinced that I was a full-blooded atheist.

A system of selling known as Multi-level Marketing (MLM) was being introduced into the UK and one participant had got hold of the mailing list for the Targeting book and sent me a postcard explaining how Bottled Water was the fastest growing market in the UK. The postcard went on to offer me an opportunity to have my own business selling water-filters, using the MLM system and building a network of other agents by recruiting and training them.

It all seemed above-board and ethical and I committed a lot of time, effort and credibility to this project. Being trusting and somewhat naive, it was a long time before I realised that most of what I had been promised, and *all* of what I was being told about other agent's sales, was grossly exaggerated – if not downright lies. I pulled out – but not before I had been badly burned financially and mentally.

Whilst getting myself back together, another deeply significant event occurred. I went to stay with my sister and her husband in Pembrokeshire, painting their house to earn money to pay some bills. My brother-in-law ran a diving school and had a fast boat with an outboard motor. One afternoon my sister asked me, 'Would you like to come and swim with *our* dolphin?'

It seemed that a wild dolphin had decided to live in a nearby bay and loved to swim and play in the water with humans and was known locally as 'Simo'. I was kitted out with a wetsuit and we motored out in the boat from the village of Solva to find him. We had gone less than a mile before Simo was sporting in our wake and when we anchored he swam around, obviously inviting us to join him. Bottle-nosed dolphins are big – Simo was about fourteen feet long and more than twice the girth of a human. In my experience up to that time, one always had to move carefully in the presence of large creatures in case you startled them and they kicked out or otherwise hurt you.

It was not like that with Simo. There seemed to be an invisible signal coming from him which was saying, 'Don't be afraid of me. Come in and play – I won't hurt you.' There was also a feeling that I can only describe as 'dolphin-love' radiating from him. I dropped over the side and he swam all around, diving down and leaping over my sister and me for about half an hour until I was tiring and swam to a nearby rock where I sat, half-submerged, to rest. Simo came and laid his head in my lap whilst my brain crackled with his attempts to communicate with me. Without a common language, all I could do was try and reciprocate the waves of love flowing around me. It was a day that has influenced my thoughts and beliefs ever since. I would wholeheartedly agree with the statement, 'Swimming with a dolphin is a life-altering experience'.

Part One. Chapter Three

Writing.

I was now 55 years old and feeling battered by the world but, buoyed by my experience with Simo, I managed to get back in with the conservatory company and, on one of my sales visits, I met a man, Aeron Clement, who, at the same age as I was, had written a book called *The Cold Moons*. This book, with badger characters, had become a best seller and earned him, so he told me, half a million pounds. This really made me think! When I was a boy on the farm my role was to control vermin, especially rabbits, rats, pigeons and grey squirrels. I had carried a .22 rifle with me much of the time and had become a competent marksman, although I never shoot animals or birds now.

Whilst hunting wild creatures one does learn a great deal about their habits and lifestyles, and I had always recognised the parallel between the way the American grey squirrels had taken over from the native red squirrels in the U.K., with the way we arrogant Europeans had taken over land and territories from native people all around the world. I decided to write a book myself, somewhat in the style of the badger book but with squirrel characters and a colonisation theme. I unleashed my imagination and wrote busily during the time when I was not visiting customers or designing their conservatories and, after a couple of false starts, the book, *The Silver Tide*, flowed out of my mind and on to the page.

The story is set in Dorset in the early 1960s and follows the adventures of a community of Red squirrels as they are forced by colonising Greys to leave their homes around the beautiful Blue Pool and eventually find refuge on Brownsea Island in Poole Harbour – 'where their descendants live to this day'.

You may recall that I was thinking of myself as a full-blooded atheist at this time and I was very surprised to find that my Red squirrel characters were not. They saw the Sun as their god and all their actions were designed to be in tune with what they perceived the Sun required of them and who, in return, provided for their needs. The Reds lived according to wise sayings known to them as *Kernels of Truth*. A typical one is

The life-giving Sun
Provides all we need. Father
Of all the squirrels.

Many of you may recognise the 5–7–5 syllable pattern of the Japanese haiku verse in the above. Another Kernel, which is a favourite of mine, relates to the burying of nuts in the autumn –

One out of eight nuts
Must be left to germinate
Here grows our future.

In the story, when a red squirrel dies the others bury it at the foot of the dead one's favourite tree, saying the Farewell Kernel –

Sun, take this squirrel
Into the peace of your earth
To nourish a tree.

Unlike the Reds, the Grey squirrels were only concerned with grabbing and holding territories for themselves. They mocked the beliefs of the peace-loving Reds and modified their own behaviour in line with edicts from their current chief, known as The Great Lord Silver, who resided in the Oval Drey at Woburn until he was deposed by a stronger rival.

More and more I found environmental and Christian beliefs infiltrating the story. The Reds had in their group a story-teller named Dandelion. When the occasion was appropriate, she told stories to the other squirrels and I was intrigued to find that her stories were mostly from the Christian Bible – with squirrels playing the main roles rather than humans.

Other authors will tell you that, once their fictitious characters are established, the characters take on lives of their own. It is unwise to try and tell the characters what to do – they just won't do it. You, the author, give them a personality, set them in a situation and then write down what you see them doing and what you hear them saying.

When *The Silver Tide* was finished I had the usual difficulties that new writers have in finding a publisher. However, it was eventually published and sold some 30,000 copies in English, Dutch, Danish and German.

By the time I had finished the sequel, *The Second Wave*, and a third squirrel book, *The Golden Flight*, to make up a trilogy, I found that I was no longer comfortable in calling myself an atheist and asked myself, 'Was I now a Christian?'

I remembered, from my confirmation classes, that the Nicene Creed, which had been first compiled in 325 A.D., listed all the things in which Christians are supposed to believe and looked up a copy. The text struck me as archaic and mostly irrelevant to a real belief. No! – if I had to believe all that I was definitely not a Christian! And yet, having heard my squirrels retell the bible stories I had learned from the nuns so long ago, it struck me that Jesus had got so much right. I knew I couldn't now call myself an atheist but I was *not* a Christian, despite a growing love for the teachings of Jesus. Here was another dilemma – I could not say 'Jesus Christ' as the word Christ means *The Messiah* or the *Son of God*, which I was not prepared to accept. I therefore always use the term 'Jesus of Nazareth' to denote the man whom I love and respect for his teachings, even though he died some two thousand years ago.

I was still working at conservatory design as the books had not produced the income that many people believe comes from being a published author. In each of the Squirrel books there were dolphins who, based on my experience with Simo, communicated with the squirrels by telepathy. My readers were asking for more books and told me how much they loved the dolphins in the first three. I therefore decided to write a book that later became known as *Dolphin Song.*

My only experience of dolphins had been that single magical day with Simo, so I set out to learn more. Simo himself had disappeared and it was feared that he had been killed by a ship's propeller, a real hazard to friendly dolphins. However, I had learned of another who had lived for several years in the harbour-mouth at Dingle, a small town in County Kerry in western Ireland and was known locally as Fungie. *Dolphin Song* was to have both dolphin and human characters and I had decided that one of the humans, Mary, a girl in her late teens, was to visit Ireland where she would swim with Fungie.

In the story, Mary had been brutally mugged near her home in London and she was going to Dingle in the hope that Fungie could in some way help her recover from her trauma. She was to travel by ferry and bus and stay in a hostel and so, to learn at firsthand what she would experience, I too travelled by ferry and bus and stayed in a hostel. I duly swam with Fungie, once again enjoying the dolphin-love that radiated from him. Now I needed to find a way for him to pass an important message to Mary – but how?

I had already used telepathy between the squirrels and the dolphins in the earlier books and needed something different. This was the first time I really experienced what I now know as Synchronicity. It is something beyond both coincidence and serendipity. I define it thus: *When you have set yourself on a benign path the most amazing things happen to help you along that path – but you must be receptive enough to recognise what is being provided.*

(In his book – *Synchronicity* – Joseph Jaworski defines it as 'When we each discover our own destiny, synchronicity enters our journey and assists us in realizing our mission'.)

At the time I did not even know I was on a benign path, just that my book might help people recognise dolphins for the wonderful creatures that they are and I might play some part in protecting whales and dolphins from exploitation.

I was sitting on the base of an elegant dolphin statue on the harbour-side in Dingle town, wondering how I might get my Fungie character to communicate with Mary in my story. Interspecies communication was to be a key element in *Dolphin Song* and I wanted this aspect to be really original.

As I sat there musing, a minibus pulled up and stopped just next to me with a sign on the windscreen advertising 'A tour of the ancient and historic sites of the Dingle Peninsular'. Without apparently making a decision, I stood up and got onto the bus and was soon on a circular route through the magnificent coastal and mountain scenery. The first stop was near a standing stone which had horizontal and diagonal lines cut up to and across, one corner. 'Those lines make up Ogham writing,' the driver explained. 'It is named after Ogham, the Irish god of eloquence.'

I loved the idea of having a god of eloquence, it was so wonderfully Irish, and wanted to know more. It seemed that Ogham writing was devised well over a thousand years ago and each letter of the Irish alphabet could be portrayed by up to four lines on one side or other of a vertical line, with some crossing over that line. The other lines could be horizontal or diagonal, as I had seen, and could be read by those familiar with Ogham as easily as you are reading this.

When I had been delivered back to my starting point on the harbour-side I thought that it was time I bought a present for my wife, left behind in Wales. The obvious present from Dingle would be a pair of dolphin shaped ear-rings and I went into a nearby jeweller's shop to buy a pair for her. To my surprise and consternation, in a town with its tourist industry dominated by a dolphin, there were no such ear-rings for sale!

Whilst I was waiting at the counter, I picked up a leaflet which offered a service in creating individual ear-rings carrying a message in Ogham writing and this could be done, 'While you wait and watch'. The leaflet also showed how Ogham writing could be translated and, needless to say, I ordered a pair and watched in a backroom as a young man engraved the lines declaring my love on two slivers of silver. On leaving the shop with the ear-rings in my pocket I felt myself being drawn irresistibly past the quays with their moored boats and on along the side of the estuary to the harbour-mouth and as far as the lighthouse on the point. From here I could look down on anchored boats and the swimmers who were enjoying the company of Fungie.

As I watched, a fishing boat came down the channel from the town, leaving a straight line of bubbles in its wake. I imagined Fungie swimming through this wake in patterns which would replicate Ogham writing and I knew at once that here was the answer to my need.

Funded by my earnings from the conservatory business, I made other research trips to prepare me for writing *Dolphin Song*, notably to the Faroe Islands where pilot whales, which are a species of large dolphins, were still being killed in their hundreds each year, and to Vancouver Island where I observed killer whales close-up from a two-man kayak.

On a whale-watching trip in the Azores, not only did I swim with a bottle-nosed dolphin mother and her calf but watched in awe as huge sperm whales surfaced and dived not far from the boat. Perhaps the most memorable experience on that trip was when hundreds of dolphins were spotted heading towards us, leaping and diving in the sparkling sun-path, obviously joyful at finding us and relishing the opportunity to take turns at riding our bow-wave. Their joy was infectious and I lay on the foredeck, my head over the side, only a few feet from the nearest and looking directly into its huge eye. Somehow it drew me into its joyousness and projected what I can only describe as intense Love in my direction. This magical experience lasted for several minutes, then at some signal, unseen or unheard by me, they were gone. All dolphin experiences leave one with a sense of privilege and after that encounter, a strange spiritual glow stayed with me for hours.

When writing the squirrel books I had to imagine the details of their culture and their life patterns, based on my observations of squirrel behaviour. That was relatively easy to do for land-based creatures that I had been watching for most of my life. With dolphins it was much more difficult. Dolphins and, as I learned later, elephants, live in groups consisting of females and their young, with the males living more solitary lives. What did come across most strongly was the feeling of love and joy in their lives – so much so that I changed the collective noun for a group from 'a pod of dolphins' to 'a joy of dolphins' – it seemed much more appropriate. But, as most recorded dolphin behaviour has been learned only from watching captive animals, I had considerable scope in imagining their culture as wild creatures.

Although I was unaware of it at the time of writing, my spiritual journey was still progressing. One of the leading human characters in *Dolphin Song*, Mary had been brought up as a devout Roman Catholic but had lost her faith after her mugging. In her anger at God for having allowed this to happen, she rejects him and then finds her life empty and bleak. As the author, I set Mary down in Dingle and watched and reported as her involvement with Fungie and other dolphins guides her back to a position of belief and fulfilment.

My own involvement with dolphins also made me realise how arrogant we humans are to believe that we are the only really intelligent creatures on this planet. I discovered this perceptive passage in Douglas Adams' *A Hitch-hikers Guide to the Galaxy* –

It is an important and popular fact that things are not always what they seem. For instance, on the planet Earth, man has always assumed he was much more intelligent than dolphins because he had achieved so much – the wheel, New York and so on – while all the dolphins had ever done was muck about in the water having a good time. But conversely, the dolphins had always believed they were more intelligent than man – for precisely the same reasons.

Dolphin Song emerged from my mind, via my computer, over some two years. I took the finished draft, which was some 160,000 words long, to my editor, who had told me that the squirrel books had 'done well' and that she 'was looking forward to seeing *Dolphin Song*'. Imagine my horror at being told, without her having read the story, that she wanted me to cut its length to 40,000 words and target it at a readership of children. I refused and, when I later gave my reasons, explained that it was like being told by a film company that they would star my daughter in a film − if only I would cut her arms and legs off!

Part One. Chapter Four.

Selling Events and the Elephant Book.

After walking out on my publisher I was sure that I would have no difficulty in finding another but once again it proved difficult and so I decided to self-publish *Dolphin Song*. It is easy to self-publish a book but hard to find sales outlets – bookshops, especially the big chains, just do not want to know. I hit on the idea of selling my books from a stall at events such as Agricultural Shows and Gift Fairs. There I would meet my readers, use my selling skills and retain the share of the price usually taken by publishers and bookshops – and it worked – for a while.

I recovered all the rights to the three squirrel books and using the business name, Cadno Books, republished them as a single volume, *The Dorset Squirrels*, whilst also publishing *Dolphin Song* in both hardback and paperback. My first *event* was The Great Dorset Steam Fair, held annually at the end of August. I had a stall in the craft marquee and sold, over five days, some £4,500 worth of books! Had I cracked the selling problem? I thought so and for the next four or five years, split my time between conservatory work, selling books at events, and researching and writing another novel with human and elephant characters.

During this creative stage I realised that I was now seeking the truth about God and had my first real break-through after I read a book called *The Bible Code*. In it the author, Michael Drosnin, claimed to have devised a code-breaking program for his computer which, when applied to the Torah (the first five books of the Old Testament) in their original language, gave dramatic prophesies for the present time and the near future. What were most impressive were the prophesies for the last few hundreds of years which *had* come true. I am not going to go into detail here as you can read the book yourself but it seemed that, if true, there would need to be massive Super-Intelligence of some kind *here on Earth* that could predict such events. But if there were such a presence, where was it?

I put aside *The Bible Code* book and let my mind play with possibilities. There were not many! The Internet was growing very fast at this time, linking people all across the world into an electronic network where information and ideas were accessible to anyone, any-where, who was on-line. I even heard that it was possible for an operator to use spare capacity on *any* of the connected computers to create a massive super-computer capable of incredibly complex tasks, even without the operators of the individual computers knowing. I never found out if this was true or just Science Fiction – but it didn't matter. Here was my clue! Suppose this Super-Intelligence was the spare capacity in the brains of all or some of the humans on the planet working together – without their *owners* being aware of it! I pushed at this idea and it kept on working. It is probably not original – but it was to me – original *and* exciting.

If true, it cracked one of my main objections to the existence of a credible god. A Super-Intelligence like that was in effect a god and, being here on Earth, instead of 'bigger than the Universe', could take an interest, even a loving interest, in the welfare of me and everyone else.

Could I be on the right track? Like so many people before me through the ages, I wanted a personal indication from God before I was convinced. At that time, I was living near the small town of Crickhowell in Powys and often walked alone up to a natural amphitheatre in the mountain behind my house. This place has a very holy atmosphere and I believe the two unusual stone structures there are the remains of sixth-century monks' cells such as I had seen on the Dingle peninsular in Ireland.

When the glaciers of the Ice Age had retreated there would have been a lake in the hollow below the cliffs but, over millennia, this had filled itself in with moss until it formed what my grandchildren called the Humpy Bog. I walked up to the Humpy Bog one day when the ravens were calling from the cliffs and the pair of peregrine falcons who nest there were whistling to each other as they circled overhead. It was sunny and hot and I stripped down to my shorts as I walked, my mind relaxed and my body warm and comfortable. Finding a convenient stone to sit on, I sat there in the almost perfect silence of the hills wondering how I could receive an indication of the existence of such a god. I was unhappy with the *name* 'God' as it carried all the baggage of my past indoctrination and was linked with heaven and hell, bigger than the Universe, all seeing, all hearing, judging, punishing and similar negative connotations. Silently my mind cried out, 'Please, give me a name I can use instead of God.'

The reply came immediately. I cannot say if it was audible or just in my head but it was positive and unmistakable – '**Mana**'.

I played with the word. Manna was the biblical food from heaven in the Old Testament book of Exodus. Man was the root of the words mankind, human and woman. Mandate was an order or granting of authority. I sat there stunned for a while and then walked home in what I later called a *state of grace*. Colours were more brilliant, I seemed to be walking a foot off the ground and, seeing some rabbits, I wondered how I ever used to kill creatures like those and vowed that I would never do so again.

Back at my house I looked up the word 'Mana' in my dictionary and read that it was a Polynesian word for '*a concept of a life force, believed to be seated in the head, and associated with high social status and ritual power*'. I then recalled being given a small piece of jade greenstone whilst I was in New Zealand by an (adopted) Maori niece and her telling me it had good 'mana' which I had interpreted as *lucky*. Had my mind just dredged this word up and pushed it forward to satisfy my request? I didn't think it was that and I still don't in view of so many other things I have experienced since that day. I was confident that I *was* on the right track, although I needed to crack the *all mighty* puzzle, i.e. if God/Mana was *all mighty*, and was an intelligence formed from the brains of many (or all) human beings working together in some mysterious way, why did he allow terrible things to happen here on Earth? An answer was not immediately forthcoming.

I concentrated on the new book I was writing, later to be named *God's Elephants*. I have always loved elephants; they are such caring creatures and, unless provoked, very gentle. It is a terrible indictment of humans that we have reduced the population of elephants in Africa from some six million in about 1900 to just a tenth of that number by the end of the last century. This means that we have killed some 90% of all African elephants either to steal their teeth or because we wanted to plant crops on the land which up until then had been theirs! I hoped that my new book would help people see what wonderful creatures they are and play some part in protecting those that remain.

Having lived in Africa during my R.A.F. service and having seen elephants in Kenya and Tanzania, I naturally set my story on that continent and needed to revisit to see more wild elephants and to remind myself of the scenery, the sounds, the scents and the atmosphere. Over the next four years, whilst still earning my living by designing conservatories and selling books at events, I made four month-long trips, firstly to Namibia, then to Kenya, then to South Africa and Botswana and finally to Tanzania.

I had originally planned to set the story in Namibia but found that Kenya and Tanzania were more appropriate as Kilimanjaro, on the border of these two countries, became central to the story. Once again my characters soon took over and all I had to do was report what they were doing and saying. By now I was not so surprised when the elephants turned out to be deeply spiritual and the leading female character, a young tuskless elephant named Temba Kidogo, was a 'seeker of the truth'. Temba Kidogo had been orphaned as a baby, and cared for at the elephant orphanages in Nairobi and Tsavo until she returned to the wild, knowing only of human ideas and not those of wild elephants. Not surprisingly, the elephants call their god 'Mana'.

Part One. Chapter Five.

Inspiration and Making Rain.

Although extremely busy, I could not let go of the conundrum, 'If God/Mana is here on Earth and is *all mighty*, why does he let terrible things happen here?' Having, as I believed, found a key to Omar Khayyam's locked door, in that God/Mana was *not* bigger than the Universe, but could exist here and now on Planet Earth, I sought to find a way to pierce the veil through which *Omar* 'could not see'.

The linking of 'Almighty' to the word 'God' is so innate in our culture that the two words were almost impossible to separate in my mind and yet it was only by so doing that I could see through that all-obscuring veil. In *God's Elephants* the seeking youngster, Temba Kidogo, asks one of the older elephants about this.

> *'Humans kill many tembos'* [elephants] *the old one said. 'Though why Mana allows this, I fail to understand.'*
>
> *'Surely Mana could stop them,' Kidogo said. 'If Mana is the same as the humans' God, then he is* all mighty *and can do anything and stop anything.'*
>
> *'How do you know the humans' God is all mighty?' the old one asked.*
>
> *'They say* Almighty God *when they speak of him.'*
>
> *'That sounds like Yellow Tusk* [old time bad elephants] *talk. If you say something often enough and loud enough, others will accept it as a Truth. We do* not *believe that Mana is all mighty – otherwise he would not need* us *to work his plans for him.*

When I started to write fiction I was taught to ask the 'What if ?' question. What if this character falls in love with that one? What if this person loses all their money? The author then explores what might happen in these circumstances. I posed this question to myself. 'What if God/Mana is *not* all mighty?'

This led me down a most exciting chain of thought. If God/Mana was loving, as I felt sure he was, but not *all mighty,* that could account for many, or all, 'bad things' happening here on Earth. We have been conditioned to believe that God could arrange things His Way with a kind of magic wand – and have then been puzzled as to why he allows wars, earthquakes and tsunamis to kill thousands of innocent people and why he allows cancers and other illnesses to blight the lives of individuals and their families.

Take away the magic *all mighty* wand and it starts to fit together again. God/Mana might hate these things as much as we do – but can't do anything about them! Or can he?

There may be no magic wand but that doesn't mean that he is powerless. If he *is* a Super Intelligence comprised of the combined intelligences of all, or some, of us humans, then he is in a position to try and get at least a percentage of individual humans to do what he wants – and there is a very well established word for this – Inspiration! Could it be that God/Mana *inspires* selected humans to do things that could eventually result in the ending of wars, the elimination of cancer and other things which spoil the enjoyment of life for so many people? The idea fitted. We all know of people who have been *inspired* to spend their lives in laboratories studying ways of eliminating a range of illnesses and diseases – most notably successful in putting an end to the scourge of smallpox.

Others have devoted much of their lives to peacemaking and diplomatic efforts to avoid or to end wars, and others to raising money to support these front-line scientists and diplomats. My favourite charity is *The Smile Train*, an organisation that carries out facial operations on children in developing countries to correct cleft palates and hare-lips. The doctors, nurses and those who support them financially, are surely *inspired* in their efforts to enable these youngsters to smile for the first time in their lives.

My dictionary says that the word 'inspiration' comes from a Latin word meaning 'to breathe in' but I believe it could possibly be a corruption of 'inspiritation' – a spirit acting on a person.

I have avoided using the words 'spirit', 'spiritual' and 'spiritually', until now, even though they passed through my mind many times in my seeking period. For me these words carried the same kind of religious baggage as the word 'God'. Yet these are good words to describe the still mystical way in which God/Mana communicates with humans. As computers in a network communicate electronically, so God and humans can communicate spiritually.

During the period when I was researching God's Elephants, I had experienced two more examples of Synchronicity, which you may recall, I described earlier as something beyond both coincidence and serendipity and defined it thus: *When you have set yourself on a benign path the most amazing things happen to help you along that path – but you must be receptive enough to recognise what is being provided.*

The first example was fairly simple. In the early stages of planning my elephant novel, I thought that I would like to use baobab trees in my book. I was driving at the time and thinking that I knew very little about baobabs, which are not actually trees but giant succulent plants. I unconsciously reached out and turned on the car radio just as the announcer introduced a half-hour long nature programme about – baobabs!

The cynic will probably say, 'You must have heard a trailer for that programme and knew when it was coming on'. Possible, I suppose, but I was sure that I had not.

Later, during one of my research visits to Africa, I was in the Kalahari Desert in Botswana, living for a few days close to the camp of a family of Bushmen, now more correctly known as San People although they prefer the term, 'First People'. With me was a Dutch guide and interpreter, Johan, and we were welcome to visit our hosts' camp at any time and take part in, or just observe, their day-to-day activities. This Bushman experience was the highlight of that visit. We hunted porcupines with the men, gathered nuts and berries with the women and sat on the ground by their cooking fires, cracking nuts between two stones whilst the children played around us or just cuddled up to the adults. In the evening we joined in their singing and dancing around a fire just outside their camp but, during the intense mid-day heat, Johan and I would retire to our own camp to sleep through the hot afternoons.

One such afternoon I was lying on my sleeping bag outside my tent, under the shade of a large tree, wondering what special activity the elephants in my next novel could practise that would be original, interesting and would advance the story convincingly. Suddenly and without consciously willing it, I found myself walking up the hill behind our campsite, a hill covered in large rocks and baobabs. I had been in Africa long enough to have overcome the fear that behind every bush is a hungry lion and had learned that keeping alert and using reasonable care will keep you safe. I was walking quite purposely without knowing where I was going, or why, when I came to a modestly sized baobab with a stone slab at the base of its trunk. I sat down on the slab and a voice, inside my head or outside of it – once again I cannot say which – said, quite distinctly, 'Take off your clothes and stand on this stone.'

It was not a request, nor a suggestion, but definitely a *command*. I did as I had been told and stepped up onto the stone with my back to the baobab. My arms were drawn upwards and backwards against the trunk and the same voice said, 'Clear your mind and think of rain – nothing but rain'.

I stood there naked, arms back, with my head up, saying, 'Rain – Rain – Rain.'

Baobabs have fairly sparse foliage and I could see the sky above turning a greyish purple and then heard raindrops falling on the leaves above me and I could smell that distinctive 'African' smell of rain on dusty ground. How long I stood there I don't know – I was in some kind of a trance – but when I 'came to' the rain had stopped and I stepped down off the stone, dressed and walked back to the camp. For a hundred yards or so the ground was wet but after that it was as dry as it had been before. This happened in the middle of the Kalahari Desert where it had not rained for six months, if not six years! Once again I felt myself to be in that mysterious *state of grace* as I walked. Johan was still asleep when I got back to the camp and I did not tell him what had happened – I felt at that time it had been for me alone.

This synchronistic rain-making experience was *exactly* what I needed for my story when I came to write *God's Elephants* several months later. On several occasions in the book, my elephants 'make rain' in much the same way as I had done in the Kalahari Desert, except that they 'linque' trunks and do it as a small group.

Just as the squirrels in *The Dorset Squirrels* and the dolphins in *Dolphin Song* had led my thoughts into finding a way forward in spiritual matters, so too did my elephants. They taught me how important love is, or should be, in our lives and showed how God/Mana could inspire humans and in the book, elephants, to implement his plans for a better world.

Part One. Chapter Six.
Could It Be...?

Although I did not fully realise it at the time, attendances at my book-selling events were falling off. With rising costs, the organisers had to increase prices, both for admission by the public and for stallholders. With increased prices, fewer people attended and this forced admission and stall costs up yet again. I blamed *my* reducing sales per event on not having a new book, and worked hard on finishing *God's Elephants*, arranging the editing and printing whilst organising a mail-shot to customers who had asked to be informed when it was ready.

Income from conservatory sales was also falling off – partly because of the reduced amount of time I was spending on this aspect of my work but also due to the first icy blasts of what was later to be called The Credit Crunch and then The Recession.

Caught between a falling income and the considerable cost of producing *God's Elephants*, I was working too hard and too long and it was taking a toll on my health. Needless to say, I was not spending much thinking time on seeking what I jokingly called, 'The Meaning of Life, the Universe and Everything'. Eventually, after a spring, summer and autumn of two-, three- and four-day events each week, I collapsed physically and mentally and could do no work of any kind for over three months. For the first time in my life I had to go onto state-benefits as my pension (I was now 69) was inadequate to cover my day to day costs. Neither was I able to service the loans taken out to fund the production of the book and, six months later, I was forced to declare myself bankrupt.

I could not write, nor think deeply, especially about 'The Meaning of Life...' but was by then able to do a few hours of physical work in the garden each day and felt better for doing this. I was now living in a flat that was part of a gracious Victorian house in Abergavenny and my landlord asked if I knew of anyone who could restore a large but dilapidated greenhouse in the Walled Garden. I offered to do this myself, came off benefits and for a year worked on this project whilst I got myself back together. This work of recreating a beautiful building in an enchanted garden worked wonders for my mental and physical health! Each day I would saw and shape interesting wooden rafters and glazing bars, make and glaze new windows and frames and rebuild and rehang the original doors. In the afternoons of sunny days my wife would join me and paint all the components I had made that day.

When the project was nearing completion I found I was ready to start writing again. In the epilogue to *God's Elephants* I had written that I was currently researching the first book of a trilogy set in a world where oil had ceased to flow. As I developed the theme and realised with horror and despair what humans might do when faced with starvation and a complete breakdown of society, I felt inspired to abandon this concept and write a book offering hope instead.

I reviewed what I had learned up to that time as a *seeker*. As each idea jelled, I asked myself *'Could it be...?'* It would be arrogant to say I knew all about God and his ways but I have listed below most of the *Could it be...?* questions to which I was confident I had found answers, based on my own experiences and the inspiration I had received:-

Could it be that there is a God here on the planet Earth who is formed from the combined intelligences of all or some of the human inhabitants?

Could it be that this God is benign and wants to improve the conditions of all creatures who share this planet?

Could it be that this God uses the senses of humans to be aware of what is happening on this planet?

Could it be that this God needs humans to act in ways that will progress his plans for a better planet?

Could it be that this God is *not* all mighty and can only act through inspiring humans to behave in certain ways?

Could it be that this God is powered by an energy we call 'Love'?

Could it be that individual humans can communicate with this God and let him know their needs and, if reasonable, these wishes will be granted?

I believe that the answer to each of the above is a qualified, 'Yes.' I readily accept that not all these beliefs are fully supported in the chapters leading up to this one – but it has been necessary to severely edit the foregoing narrative so as not to get bogged down in too much detail. In Part Two I delve deeper into these questions and test the apparent answers against my personal experiences.

Stay with me.

The Ferry Boat

Part Two

Part Two. Chapter One.

Chiming Bells.

For many people, including myself, there are two main difficulties in believing in a god such as the one we had been taught about. The first difficulty, you will recall, is 'If God is bigger than the universe, how could he possibly be interested in me – a tiny speck of animation on a minor planet circling a second-class star on the fringe of just one of many huge galaxies?'

The other main difficulty is that 'If God is loving, benign and all mighty, as we had been taught, then how could he allow dreadful things to happen to blight our lives?'

I covered the second of these in Part One, Chapter Five where I concluded that God was *not* all mighty and, after personally experiencing a number of synchronistic experiences, I became convinced that God (or some benign spirit) *was* interested in **me** so it seemed that God (or a part of God) must be 'resident' here on Planet Earth.

This begged the question, if so – where was he? I will try to answer this and the other questions that follow, in Part Two.

George Orwell, in his book *Animal Farm*, made an analogy (comparison) between the horrors of a dictatorship on a fictitious farm run by pigs and the situation in communist-controlled Russia. Because most readers would have been familiar with farm animals, after reading the story they could readily appreciate how power could corrupt. The phrase, 'All animals are equal – but some are more equal than others,' is frequently quoted in this context. In a similar way, I will sometimes use analogies in the following chapters.

How does anyone know when something they are being told is true? Unfortunately, we have become accustomed to being lied to in varying degrees by many people, most notably politicians eager for our votes, unscrupulous salesmen promoting their product or media reporters and commentators who want to present a more interesting or exciting report. The saying, 'Don't let the facts spoil a good story!' comes to mind.

I can't say how much of what I am writing is *really* true. I am trying my best to record my own experiences exactly as I recall them – even some of these may have become distorted by time. But I have a test for other peoples' truths that I commend to you. Apply this test to what you are reading in this book.

Imagine that you want to buy a new bell – a big one such as you would find in a church tower. Now imagine a second-hand bell yard where dozens of such bells are displayed for sale. No matter what the salesman tells you, you won't buy a bell until you test it. You take a small hammer and tap the rim. If the bell is cracked, or otherwise faulty, it won't ring true. Put another way – it won't chime with you.

I invite you to test each of the ideas I will present in this section against your own experiences and see if they 'chime with you'. They do for me or they wouldn't have been included. Be prepared for some of them to chime in an unexpected way but, even so, you can tell if it is a true chime!

Much of what you are going to read is speculation based on what chimes for *me* and I accept that there may be many different interpretations of my experiences. If none, or few, of the ideas presented here chime for you, then this book is probably no help in *your* spiritual journey. However, I really hope that you will be saying, 'That sounds true!', 'I like that idea!', 'That could be what I have been looking for!' and other comments in this vein. If just a few of the readers call out, 'Yes, yes, YES!' or even say, 'I wish I'd known that when I was sixteen', then all the effort put into this book will have been worth it.

Part Two. Chapter Two.

The Two Main Analogies.

The question of where God was and how he could be interested in me, I described in Part One as Omar Khayyam's 'door to which I had no key'.

Having discussed this problem with other people, I found that Omar and I were far from being the only ones without that particular key.

Once I became convinced that there was a god who was able and willing to communicate with me, I needed to find an answer to the first question posed above. The only answer that made any kind of sense was for God (or a god) to be resident here on our planet Earth. If this was so, it led to another important question, 'Where on Planet Earth could that god be?'

This is the answer which chimes with me –

I would like you to think of how our bodies work. We are each of us made up of millions upon millions of minute, living cells, all cooperating to form a single body capable of performing an infinite variety of tasks from writing a letter to digging the garden, from cooking a meal to running a marathon. Various parts of our body communicate with other parts by way of the brain, which is composed of millions of a different type of cell. The brain is constantly receiving messages from the eyes, the ears, and other *sensing* cells and sometimes receives warnings of danger or damage, by way of pain. Some cells report *needs*, such as, 'Our body needs more liquid – or more food,' and the brain prioritises these needs and arranges for them to be satisfied if possible. All of these functions are so common and automatic that we hardly give a thought to the fact that they are happening at all.

Most other living creatures have bodies that perform similar tasks to our own, although plants do not have brains and, as far as we know, don't feel pain but have other methods of dealing with damage.

Higher creatures also have something we call 'intelligence' which is present in differing degrees and is a very special possession. Intelligence is hard to describe, and difficult to measure objectively, although many have tried. We are not even sure *where* it resides in our bodies but it would seem to be somewhere within our brains and, generally speaking, the bigger the brain the greater the intelligence – but not always. Some birds, notably from the crow and the parrot families, seem to display more intelligence than some animals with much bigger brains.

When we are born we have lots of brain cells but little, if any, intelligence. As children with a developing intelligence, we learn about our immediate environment – what things feel good and what don't. Our experiences are sorted by our intelligence and the results stored in our brains as memories. These memories are called on many times to direct our actions if we are in danger, to help us find food and shelter and, in the modern world, to guide us in a multitude of ways such as how we work, how we spend our money and how we manage our relationships. Even though the workings of our intelligence are not fully understood, we all have one – or we could not function at all. *I* could not be writing this book and *you* could not be reading it!

Every day vast numbers of the cells making up our bodies and brains die and are replaced by new cells. I have been told that, over several years, virtually every cell in my body has died and been replaced by others – yet I am still recognisably *me*. I look the same, walk the same, talk the same and have the same memories. I remember the same silly jokes and love the same people and things as I always have done – even when every cell in my *new* brain has replaced those that had previously made up my *old* brain.

Eventually, as a result of an accident, an illness or probably because I can no longer replace these dying cells with new ones, I will myself die and my body will return in some way to the soil for recycling – 'Ashes to ashes, dust to dust'. The bio-electrical signals in my brain will have ceased and I will be finished, dead, kaput, an ex-person! Or will I?

One of the most attractive promises made by many religious belief systems is that some vital part of us survives beyond our physical deaths. This doctrine, often seen as just a fanciful desire, turns many people away from wanting to have anything to do with religion; they perceive such a belief to be mere wishful thinking. This is especially true now that we have a better understanding of the vastness of the Universe and the unlikeliness of there being a 'paradise in the sky' known as Heaven.

When Judaism, Christianity and Islam were developing, people believed that this planet was the centre of the universe and it was quite reasonable for them to believe that we humans were the most important part of that planet and, consequentially, the most important part of the universe. It was also reasonable therefore to believe that any god that did exist, existed for us. The relatively recent knowledge that there are many billions of galaxies each made up of millions of stars, made this concept untenable.

And yet – many of us *do* feel that there is some agency, external to ourselves, who cares about us and plays a part in our lives.

We saw earlier how our intelligence, which we can neither locate nor describe exactly, but which directs our actions and emotions, must reside somewhere in the composite workings of millions of our brain cells – yet this, our intelligence, continues to function *normally and without interruption* as these individual cells die and are replaced over a period of years.

Could it be that God is a Super-being active on this planet who is made up of our brains and bodies in the same way as *we* are made up of millions of cells? And that this Super-being has an invisible intelligence which is as responsive to the needs of us (we being its cells,) as we are to the needs of the cells in our bodies?

All that I am suggesting here is a 'scaling up' of the cell/body arrangement, to a much greater size and complexity. This Super-being (God) would use our bodies and brains in much the same way as *we* use *our* component cells. We get on with what we do best (living our little lives) whilst our senses are used to keep God informed of what is happening where we are, and our brains – in conjuction with millions of others – are used by God to host an intelligence with a vast capability.

In Part One I told how I was involved with very early small computers back in the mid-1970s when processing power was in the range of 8 – 16K and the idea of linking two or more computers together was the stuff of Science Fiction. Now, less than half a century later, we have a World Wide

Web of computers accessed by billions of people, simultaneously, all around the globe. It is, as yet, the stuff of Science Fiction that these computers will one day spontaneously unite their power and develop an intelligence of their own.

Could it be that there is already a World Wide Spirit in existence of which each of us is, or could be, a part?

Back to our web of computers. If these *did* someday collaborate to form an Electronic Super-Intelligence (ESI) with a will of its own, how would this ESI set out to implement this will? The computers comprising it are themselves mostly static but are operated by humans who are capable of performing many functions. Thus if the ESI needed things to be done that could only be done by physical bodies, the ESI would instruct selected humans (via their computer terminals) to undertake the necessary actions to implement its will.

Back to our World Wide Spirit – which I am calling 'God'. If God is somehow the united intelligence of billions of humans across the planet, then each of us is, or could be, a part of God. I find this a wonderful and uplifting, but sobering, thought. Ordinary, unimportant me – a part of God! What a privilege!

I love the idea – but is it true? I can't say. But, starting from the point that it could be, I have explored many and various aspects of this possibility and they all 'hang together'.

Part Two. Chapter Three.

The Cell Analogy

Try this test. Imagine that you are one of the cells in your own body – say a nerve cell in the tip of your index finger. You have a definite role to play in the body. Your job, as a nerve cell, is to report on what you feel when the finger-tip touches some object. You may report, 'Cold', 'Hot', 'Smooth', 'Rough', 'Sticky', or a whole range of other sensations. The finger-tip has been instructed to *feel* by the brain and the reports that you (the nerve cell) make are interpreted by another part of the brain, and then compared with memories of similar experiences held in yet another part of your brain. This is all computed and assessed by your *intelligence* and signals are then sent, via the communication nerves, back to the finger-tip. These signals might say, 'Stop touching! You will be hurt,' or perhaps, 'That feels good – keep contact.' All of the above happens in a fraction of a second. If you, as a finger-tip nerve, had intelligence, would you not view the higher *intelligence* as some kind of 'god'?

I offer this analogy to make the point that the finger-tip nerve *knows* what to do – its job is to report what it senses. It is the job of *other* cells to act on what the report says.

In my *human body as a part of God* analogy, if its cells (representing we humans) didn't know how to report or how to act when we received instructions, then God could not function effectively. And this is the current situation! *Most* people don't report, or act on instructions, because they either don't know they can or because they are too self-centred to do so. In the above analogy, if the finger-tip nerve felt 'hot' but did not report this, or the finger-tip muscle cells did not pull the finger away, then a vital part of the body would be harmed. Of course an *all mighty* God wouldn't need us to do this anymore than an *all mighty* body would need nerves or muscles. However, if we accept one of the main pillars of my proposition (i.e. that God is **not** all mighty – more on this later,) then he needs as many of us to be acting on his behalf as possible.

In the previous chapter I mused on the privilege of being a part of God in his form as a World Wide Spirit. Shortly I will show how, if we choose to, we can become his eyes, ears and other senses, consciously or unconsciously feeding back our observations and then implementing the instructions we receive. All that is needed is for us to be 'plugged in' and receptive.

However, if we accept that God is here on Earth with us and not 'bigger than the Universe' as I was taught, then this begs the question, 'So who or what controls things on a Universal scale?'

I don't pretend to have an answer to that – at present it is enough for us to find out what *our* God here on Planet Earth expects from us and try and implement his will. In the analogy above, would we expect our finger-tip nerves to ask what *our* ultimate purpose was?

If you think that this a 'cop out' on my part, I am quite prepared for that but I did not set out to explain the workings of the whole Universe. It is more than enough for me to try and understand our place on this wonderful planet and to share my conclusions with you.

I have always been puzzled by the concept of 'free will', embodied in Christianity and some other established faiths, i.e. that each human has the right to do whatever they choose in relation to God. In our modern world, we have given up our right to 'free will' in relation to other people within the society in which we live, and we conform to rigid rules of behaviour or we would end up in prison – and rightly so. Society would not function effectively if we all exercised our right to free will in this respect. Neither can God function effectively if we take advantage of 'free will' to behave as selfishly as we might wish.

What I am proposing is that we just share with God what we are experiencing – what we see, what we hear, and what we feel, as well as sharing our joys, our sorrows, our fears and our pleasures. Then, when we receive instructions by way of our consciences or what we call 'gut-feelings', we should act on these instructions as best we can. Traditional 'western' religions seem to me to have restricted our *consciences* to just telling us what not to do (e.g. Thou shalt not kill,) I am sure that this is inadequate and we should expect *positive* messages as well.

There is a danger of a misunderstanding in the foregoing. When I talked of reporting what we see, etc. to God and then go on to talk about society, I do not want to suggest that we report the misdemeanours of *other people* to God – that would make us like the infamous STASI secret police of the G.D.R. – the now nonexistent communist-led German Democratic Republic.

61

Part Two. Chapter Four.

Inspiration and ISPs

Remember Omar Khayyam's second problem? *'There was a Veil through which I might not see...'*

To me this was the question, 'If God is here on Earth and is *all mighty*, why does he let terrible things happen to us?'

As this is a question that perplexes so many people trying to come to terms with the existence of a god, I will return to it here.

The linking of 'Almighty' to the word 'God' is so innate in our culture that the two words were almost impossible to separate in my mind and yet it was only by so doing that I believed I could see through that all-obscuring veil.

If God was loving but not *all mighty,* that could account for many 'bad things' happening here on Earth, as he would be powerless to prevent them in the short term. In the longer term, he could act to reduce or eliminate these by *inspiration.* We discussed how God/Mana could inspire people to work his will and act selflessly to combat cancers and other illnesses and to act as peace-keepers. These selfless acts also cover devoting time and effort to charitable causes and generally 'doing good' for the benefit of the planet and all its inhabitants.

There has been much discussion recently about Genetically Modified (G.M.) plants and animals which have been given the provocative name of 'Frankenstein Foods' by certain newspapers. It seems that it is now possible for sections of the DNA code of plants and animals to be removed from one and 'spliced' into the seed of another.

When I first read about this happening, I was uneasy about it but, after developing the 'inspiration' idea outlined above, I have changed my view. I am particularly interested in the work being done to enable crops such as wheat to 'fix' nitrogen in their roots in the same way as clover, peas and beans do, thus being able to capture their nitrogen needs from the air rather than having this supplied by the farmers in the way of expensive additional fertilizers.

Farmers, stockbreeders and plant breeders have for centuries been modifying animals, birds and plants by selective crossbreeding to produce better offspring – mostly 'better' in terms of more productive for human consumption. This has generally been seen to be acceptable and not unnatural and has enabled harvests of crops such as wheat and rice to be increased many times. This has to be beneficial for feeding a growing population. Could it be that those people were inspired to develop the superior animals and plants by God/Mana? They may have been unaware of it at the time and just thought of improving farming profits or even personal prestige. Could it be that the development of G.M. crops is the result of a similar inspiration?

If God/Mana is inspiring humans to do his will then it would be good to have a closer look at who this God might be. I am sure that God is fundamentally benign, for which I have no explanation other than I cannot find any sense in the existence of a malign or vengeful God, nor in a 'planet-restricted' God who does *not* have the welfare of this planet and it inhabitants as a main concern.

If we accept (at least for the moment) that there *is* a God comprising the intelligences of all (or many) of the humans on this planet, is this the Three-in-One God of the Christians, Jehovah (YHVH) of the Jews, Allah of the Muslims, Ik Onkar of the Sikhs, or perhaps one of the many Gods of the Hindus? My simple answer is 'Yes, he is *all* of these,' and I realise that this statement will upset many practitioners of religions who have been brought up to believe that *their God* is the only 'true' God and all others are false.

One of the difficulties these people will have in opening their minds to the idea that they could *all* be right, is that so many of their leaders, over so many centuries, have developed a vested interest in promoting their version of God above all others. In some parts of the world and in various periods of history, the penalties for having an even slightly different belief have been draconian, even fatal.

Let's return to our World Wide Web analogy for a moment. Imagine that you have just bought your first computer. You ask the shop assistant, or more likely a friend or work colleague, which company they would recommend as an ISP (Internet Service Provider) to give you access to the Internet. They could say 'British Telecom,' or 'AOL (America on Line)' or 'TalkTalk' or one of dozens of others but, if it is a friend you are asking, it is probable that they would say, 'I use XYZ,' (whatever that happens to be). *You* then register with XYZ and use that ISP to access the internet for whatever purpose. You may later find that another ISP suits you better as it may give faster access or not display so many advertisements, but whichever you do use, it will still access *the same Internet.*

So it happens with the different religions! If you are born into a Roman Catholic family, you will almost certainly be baptised and brought up as a Roman Catholic but, if you were born next door, to a family of Methodists, you would most likely be brought up as a Methodist. Next door again and you might well find that you are brought up as a Sikh and, if you are male, expected to wear a turban and other accoutrements all your life. Surely, in their purest sense, all of these religions are just ISPs to the same God?

Part Two. Chapter Five.

Joy and Love.

A benign God who is concerned about the welfare of this 'his' planet and its inhabitants would need to be powered in some way. Just as computers are powered by electricity, I speculate that God is powered by that difficult to define, but very real, power we call 'Love'. This is a fairly wild speculation with, as far as I know, no scientific basis. I may be completely wrong here and, if I am, it does not matter overall. It is interesting to follow the idea through, because there may be some truths within it.

It is possible for forms of energy to exist of which we are totally unaware. For instance, two hundred years ago radio waves and microwaves were unknown and even electricity was observed only in flashes of lightning and when one's hair stood on end when brushed vigorously. Now electricity and electronics are understood more fully and power huge areas of our lives, from lighting and heating, to computers and telephones. It is a sobering thought that, only a few centuries ago, if you had demonstrated with a mobile phone that you could talk directly to someone in the next town, ten miles away, let alone in America or Australia, you could have been burned at the stake as a witch or a servant of the devil!

So, if Love is the mystic force that empowers God, where might this Love come from?

Scientists have been puzzled in that they have calculated (don't ask me how) that there should be much more energy/matter in the Universe than there appears to be. Their calculations leave some 94% unaccounted for and they have named this missing substance 'Dark Matter'. Could it be that this Dark Matter is the raw material of Love?

Dark Matter is a very negative name; I suggest we call it *Divine Energy* and picture this as filling the Universe in an invisible and (as yet) an immeasurable form. Could it be that living creatures here on Earth have the ability to capture and condense this Divine Energy and turn it into Love? What a wonderful idea!

When we think deeply about Love we realise that it has a unique property – unlike chocolate cake, Love multiplies when shared; e.g, a returned smile does not deplete the stock of Love of either party but seems to increase it for both. The more you think about it and relate this to one's own experiences, the truer it seems.

In Part One I told of the Joy and Love I experienced when swimming with the dolphin, Simo, and also of being the recipient of the Love of joyous dolphins around me when lying on the deck of a yacht when sailing near the Azores.

I realise now that Joy and Love seem to be linked and that Love is somehow created *from* Joy. Could it be that Dark Matter/Divine Energy is actually the raw energy received by living creatures here on Earth and expressed as Joy? The more I explore the idea, the more it seems to 'hang together'. A receptive creature (a human, a dolphin or perhaps an elephant), experiences Joy from some pleasant activity or situation, and converts it into Love, which it can share with others of its kind or, as with my experiences in West Wales and the Azores, even between species. Could it be that other life-forms, or even inanimate objects, for example the trees in a wood or the rocks of a mountain, might be able to absorb this Divine Energy and create a *spirit of the wood* or a *spirit of the mountain*? I certainly have experienced such feelings and they are closely akin to Joy. I would then be moved to say, 'How I love that wood', or 'How I love that mountain'.

Let's follow through the idea that Divine Energy/ Potential Joy is everywhere waiting to be tapped. As we enjoy ourselves, in whatever form, we build up a store of Love within ourselves which we can project, as in a smile or a caress, and share with others. As we *share* this Love, we experience more Joy from the sharing and this increases our *stock* of Love. Some people (my mother was a prime example) have a huge stock of Love to share and they do so readily with whoever they meet. Could it be that this Love, created from Joy, is the force which energises God – the World Wide Spirit – in the same way that electricity energises the World Wide Web through the computers that constitute it?

Christians have a saying, 'God is Love,' which had puzzled me for most of my life. Could it be that God receives our Love and returns it to us in a magnified form ? If this is true and Love is created from Joy, which in turn is condensed from Divine Energy, then the full cycle would be:-

Divine Energy (Dark Matter/Potential Joy) is present throughout the Universe in vast quantities but in a very rarefied state?

Humans (and possibly other creatures such as dolphins and elephants) can capture and condense this Divine Energy into Joy.

This Joy can be converted into Love and stored within oneself and shared with others.

When shared, this Love becomes multiplied, (possibly by drawing in more raw Divine Energy), and used as a power source by God.

This Love is magnified by God and returned to us.

As I commented at the start of this chapter, this is all (wild) speculation but it could be the answer to the question, 'What powers God.'

Part Two. Chapter Six.

Truth and Beauty.

Whilst we are in a 'fanciful' mood, let's explore another related area which is also difficult to define.

'Beauty is truth, truth beauty. That is all ye know on Earth and all ye need to know.'
When I first read these lines by the poet Keats, they moved me greatly, even though at the time, I did not understand what they were saying.

Consider the words and the meanings of *Truth* and *Beauty* – as with *Joy* and *Love*, we have no unit of measurement for them. In the previous chapter, we discussed the idea that Divine Energy (Dark Matter/Potential Joy) permeates the Universe and can be captured and condensed by humans and possibly by other creatures. Could it be that Divine Energy is also the raw energy for creating Truth and Beauty?

In my dictionary, Truth is defined as, 'The quality of being true, genuine, actual or factual,' and Beauty is defined as, 'The combination of the qualities of a person or thing that delight the senses and please the mind'.

I feel that both these definitions are inadequate! Both Truth and Beauty have a higher, more spiritual meaning – a kind of absolute standard – an essence of extreme *rightness* that is beyond the creation of humans alone.

Real Truth and Beauty can be found in the work of artists, writers, poets and composers of music. Could it be that, where ordinary humans can capture and *condense* Divine Energy into Joy and convert this into Love, truly creative people can capture and *distil* Divine Energy into great and beautiful paintings, sculptures, poems, music, architecture, engineering and mathematics? From my own experiences and observations, this distillation process is immensely energy-draining and is achieved only through the utmost dedication to one's art. However, the energy and detailed effort invested in the painting, poem or other creative work, can induce Joy and create Love in many other people, both at the time of its creation and for generations to come.

As a writer, (and I do regard this fact as a great privilege) I have a responsibility to present the truth as I see it for others to taste, savour and then to accept or reject.

As a poet, (an even greater privilege) I accept an even larger responsibility for identifying important issues (truths?), teasing out their deeper meanings and presenting these to other people in a form that is both beautiful and precise and one that will be welcomed and understood. I believe absolutely that if a listener or reader does not grasp the fundamental message or expression of feeling, the first time they hear or read a poem, the poet has not worked hard enough on their behalf!

Often the poet's function is to speak on behalf of those who are not so adept at recognising these truths for what they are.

Poets just express
What other people feel but
Can't articulate.

and

Poets must express
What other people feel but
Can't articulate.

Not being at all musical, I can't speak for composers, but I am told by those who are musical that great music is full of 'truths' and is as uplifting to their spirits as great poetry is to mine.

I also know from writing my 'wildlife' novels that, when you abandon yourself and let the characters lead you on, you can learn truths that you didn't know you knew! It even gets to the point that, when you read back over the manuscript, you have no recollection of having written various passages – especially the most perceptive ones.

All beauty is not man-made – in fact most occurs naturally, from an awe-inspiring landscape to the exquisite beauty of even the smallest flower or butterfly.

One of my favourite flowers is the Amaryllis which is certainly not a *small* flower. I first saw an Amaryllis when I visited a friend's house whilst in my teens and thought it to be a rather ugly 'showing-off' flower. More recently I was given a bulb to grow myself. It was huge when compared with that of a daffodil or a tulip and it sat in its pot on my bedroom window-sill without any sign of life whilst I watered it hopefully every couple of days. Then, with a majestic slowness, a bud appeared on one side of the crown and, drawing on the life-giving water, it grew up and up whilst a second bud appeared on the other side of the crown. This new bud waited, without further movement, whilst the first one took days to expand before breaking open to reveal four glorious blood-red, trumpet-shaped flowers.

When I lay in bed, I could see the whole plant silhouetted again the sky outside and became aware of the exquisitely elegant curve of the stem and the dramatic outlines of the flowers. This had been Act One in the drama of showing me its beauty.

As the first flowers faded and shrivelled, Act Two commenced. The second bud started to grow, with an equally elegant stem, balancing the other, which was now drooping sideways. Just as the colours finally faded from the first flower, the second bud opened as dramatically as the first.

Then, for Act Three, the second flower faded and drooped just as a cluster of broad leaves with bluntly pointed ends emerged, at an imperceptible speed, from the crown of the bulb, the first leaf growing to the left and the second to the right and so on. Eventually there were some eight dark-green leaves curving over from their bases with an architectural precision that was beautiful to behold, even after the flowers and their stems had shrunk away to virtually nothing.

Finally the leaves themselves faded and dried-up one by one – but only after capturing sunlight and storing it in a rejuvenated bulb ready to repeat the performance in the following year. That brilliant natural display represented, and still does, a real beauty and a significant truth to me.

In my novel, *Dolphin Song*, I explored the question of whether there was a single Truth or if there were many different Truths. The culture of the Star-whales (Pilot Whales) of the story was that each whale sang their philosophy in a Song of Truth that could change as their situations changed. In one passage the dolphin, *Grace of FairIsle*, speaks to the pilot whale, *Nordstar,* who, together with another dolphin, *Elegance of Rockall,* are held in captivity together.

FairIsle asked Nordstar about Songs of Truth.

'They just come,' Nordstar told her.

'No. There must be rules about how they are made.'

'If there are, I was never taught them. They just come.'

FairIsle was insistent. 'If it was as simple as that, any 'phin or whale could devise one easily. Your Song was beautiful. Sad, but beautiful.'

Nordstar rose to breathe. 'The most important thing is that they tell the Truth as you see it. We spoke of this before, in the dead boat on the way here from the Eighteen Islands.'

'Tell me again,' FairIsle asked. 'I would like Rockall to hear. We would like to make a Song of our Truths.'

'Then it will be two Songs, and two Truths. No whale ever sees the same Truth. First you must find what your Truth is. When you think you have found it, surround it with a shoal of words and see which ones fit. Sometimes the words change, sometimes the Truth changes, but eventually they all swim together. Then you must sing the Song and see if it floats through the surface of the sea towards the stars. If it does not, you must work on it again and again until it does.'

'What if it never does?' Rockall asked.

'Let it sink – it is not a True Song.'

Somehow, in a way I do not understand, the concepts of a benign God, Truth and Beauty are interconnected. Perhaps God loves both but needs Humans to appreciate Truth and Beauty, either natural or man-made and needs our senses to share the resulting Joy and Love with him.

Part Two. Chapter Seven.

Ideas on Evolution.

For the forgoing to have any validity, I must suggest at least one credible way for our planet-sized god to have come into being.

This is a difficult task – but not as difficult as explaining how the Universe itself 'happened'. The latter question I cheerfully ducked on the basis that it is no concern of ours until at least we have sorted out our own situation here on Planet Earth, and I am quite ready to accept that we may never know the answer to 'The Big Questions of How and Why'. I find it incredibly arrogant to even begin to believe that we *could* understand it if we did know – and what use would this knowledge be anyway? I submit that any spare mental energy we have should be spent doing our best to assist our planet-based God work his will for the betterment of Earth and all its inhabitants.

Could it be that the seeds of Life floated in from space to a barren planet, as Earth was billions of years ago? Planet Earth must at that time been in a state where conditions were ripe for simple colonisation by 'life'. When I was writing my novel, *God's Elephants,* I was thinking about this in the dining room of a pub in Southend-on-Sea after a long and hard day selling my books at a local show. The answer came drifting into my mind as a part of a song which a whale had taught to one of my elephant characters, Tembo Lonely. In the story, the whale and the elephant had discovered that they could communicate with one another using Low~Sound, which we humans call 'Infrasound', and it is a fact that elephants use infrasound to communicate with other elephants, and whales with other whales. It only took a little author's licence to make it happen between species. (In his fascinating non-fiction book, *Elephantoms*, the author, Lyall Watson, claims to have been present when a similar phenomenon happened.)

Here is the first part of the Whale's Song from *God's Elephants* – sung to the rhythm of Longfellow's *Hiawatha*.

In the dim and distant ages
This our planet was quite lifeless.
Came a time when it was ready
Ready like a flower open,
Craving for a speck of pollen.

Floating in from where we know not
Came a drift of cosmic pollen
Carrying the sacred Life-force
To this silent, waiting planet.

Like the flower gaining pollen
Earth responded to this Life-force.
Simple plants and simple creatures
Flourished here in great abundance
Making from this sterile body
Something more than rocks and water.

Then evolution and the survival of the fittest kicks in –

As time passed these plants and creatures
Grew more complex, found their places

Leading to a wondrous richness
Making up the world around us.

On the way a million, million
Plants and creatures formed and flourished
Failed and perished, died and vanished.
Others – fitter, stronger, better,
For the role that needed playing
Took their places in this complex
Web of interactive life-forms.

It was here in the story that a god comes into being –

At some point, a mystic union
Of these plants and other creatures,
With the earth and rocks and water
Formed a being whales call 'Gaia'
Mother-being of our planet.

Gaia, *like a mother whale,*
Knew the Joy of Procreation
Knew **her** *role, to care and nourish.*
But another force was needed
With intelligence and forethought
Powered by Love – she named **him** *'Mana'.*

Gaia *chose from all her creatures*
Four to serve our planet's interests
Four to give it thought and focus
Four to save it from destruction

Here I must introduce another concept. We humans are so arrogant that few of us consider that there may well be other creatures who could be as intelligent as we are. If I am right in my belief that God is the combined intelligence of living creatures on this planet, then it is likely that all those creatures who are most capable of intelligent reckoning (beyond that needed for day to day survival,) also play an active role in the functioning of our God. From my own observations, I would firmly place whales, dolphins and elephants in this category. Other people to whom I have suggested this concept, want to extend this to domestic dogs and cats, and some to horses, tigers and bears. They could be right – but it doesn't alter the idea that God is not just reflecting and guiding *Human* thought.

The next part of the whale's song develops the concept that those creatures with the biggest brains are selected by Gaia to play the strongest roles in creating Mana, the directing God of our planet as the whales saw him.

From the oceans she chose **whales**
Great in body, great in wisdom
With a brain that could develop
Play a part in forming Mana.

As a balance she chose **dolphins**
Smaller, joyful, fond of playing
Loving freedom, kind and caring
Dolphins would be good for Mana.

Greatest on the land were **tembos**   [elephants]
Like the whales, great in wisdom

Storing in their tusks the Loving
Mana *needed for his workings.*

Lastly, Gaia *chose the* **humans**
Smaller, joyful, fond of playing
Loving freedom, kind and caring
Humans would be good for Mana.

Whales, dolphins, tembos, humans
All were granted 'beings' greater
Than their bodies, blood and brains were.
Call these 'beings' – **souls** *or* **spirits**,
Hallowing the chosen foursome.

Now a new concept was introduced into the Whale's song – that all the other plants and animals were there to provide food and other sustenance and support to the four 'big-brains' who are all at the top of the food-chain.

All the myriad other life-forms
Fill the needs of whales and dolphins,
Feed the tembos and the humans
So they can devote their lives to
Service for the good of Mana.

Link these spirits round the planet
Link the spirits of the foursome
Link the whales and the dolphins
With the tembos and the humans
Call this combined spirit– **Mana**.

Think of Gaia as **our mother**
Caring for the plants and creatures.
Think of Mana *as* **our father**
Planning for our planet's future
Seeing what needs doing.   Only –
With no hands or trunks or flippers
He needs **US** *to do what's needed.*

His the vision, ours the labour
Without *Mana,* we are nothing
Without us, he's nothing either
Mana *needs us – we need* **Mana.**

We need food to fill our bellies,
Give us strength to live and flourish,
Make more whales, dolphins, tembos
Make more humans – all are needed
To ensure that Mana *lives on.*

Our role is serving Mana
Seeking Joy in all around us
Seeking Joy and with it forming
Love, to power the work of Mana.

It's from Joy that Love emerges
Transmuted by our souls and spirits
Joy – to Love. Our gift to Mana.
He needs Love as we need fishes,
Meat or plants to fill our bellies.
It is Joy that we must cherish
Turn to Love to nourish Mana.

If we choose to take what's offered,
Giving nothing, being greedy,
Never giving Love to Mana,
Thinking that our selfish comforts
Justify our whole existence,
We will grow away from Mana.

Then our lives will be so empty
We can't ever link with Mana.
Arrogance and fear will fill us
Fear of loss and Fear of dying.
In the hearts and souls of whales
In the hearts and souls of dolphins
In the hearts and souls of tembos
 In the hearts and souls of humans.

Real Love and real caring
Take away these Fears forever.

Listen to the voice within you
That is Mana, speaking softly
Saying what you should be doing
Sometimes hard and sometimes easy.
Don't ignore that voice within you
Or Mana's plans can't reach fruition.

Mana *needs the Love we give him,*
Formed from Joy and care for others
For **Love** *is the magic power*
The force that links us all together.

Here's the wonder, here's the beauty
Here's the honour, here's the duty
We can all be part of Mana.

We will all be part of Mana
If we share the Love within us
Love that Mana needs to function
To ensure our planet's future
As a place of Truth and Beauty,
Harmony and Peace – for ever.

In writing this chapter I had not intended to quote the whole of the whale's song. However, as I tried to select which parts of it were relevant and most likely to be true, I found that more and more of it ended up on the page. Until now, I have kept the 'Gaia' concept only within the whale's song of the elephant story and not attempted to develop it in the main body of this book – but it does have a certain appeal. This would imply that there are two Gods active on this planet – Mother Gaia / Father Mana.

The earliest man-made artefacts that have been found (other than stone tools) are representations of the female figure, often bulging in pregnancy. These are held to represent the Mother Earth goddess, named Gaia by the ancient Greeks. I have no quarrel with this. Our planet has always provided support and sustenance for living creatures in much the same way as a human mother proves support and sustenance for her children.

Whether these figures were in fact venerated by their creators we cannot know but it seems likely that they were used as reminders of where the necessary things to support their lives came from.

Much later, we learn about the myth of Adam and Eve, still a part of the teachings of both the Jewish and Christian faiths. Here the woman, Eve, is created by God from a rib-bone taken from the first man, Adam. Although this story is accepted as just a myth by most people, it puzzles me that, even as a story attempting to explain to an unsophisticated society how humans came into being, the *man* came first. It would seem much more natural for the woman to have been created first and the man created from *her* rib-bone. Perhaps it was an early piece of male-supremacy propaganda!

However, most reasonable people would accept that the roles of men and women are different and complementary. Here I will say that, whilst I accept that all roles, jobs and positions in modern society should be equally accessible to both sexes, it is clear to me that men are, by build and attitude, more likely to thrive in some jobs and women to thrive in others.

In an ideal society as I see it, women provide a secure, loving and comfortable home in which they play the greater role in providing for the children's day-to-day needs, whilst the man provides immediate protection and does the major, longer term planning for the future needs of the family. Of course this statement is grossly over-simplistic – modern society is much, much more complex than this.

During the (very limited) time I was living with the San Bushmen in Botswana, it was apparent to me that this was the natural, if primitive, way. What did come across most strongly from that experience was the love for the young children expressed by both sexes through frequent, unashamed cuddling of the little ones.

The man/woman/child – Mana/Gaia/humans – relation-ship could be the subject of a whole book on its own but I mention it here because it gives us a valuable insight into how our relationship with God/Mana can be easily managed.

Think of our planet Earth and all of nature here as our Mother, Gaia, providing for our basic needs and being worthy of our respect, love and consideration.

Think of God/Mana as our Father, to whom we express our special needs in the hope and expectation that these will be satisfied if at all possible – because he loves us and wants us to have the best possible lives.

When Jesus of Nazareth was attempting to explain the God/people relationship two thousand years ago, he used the same analogy. Even his prayer, which has survived over all that time, starts, 'Our Father...'

Gaia would be the 'Mother Goddess' who developed the life of all creatures here on Planet Earth from simple life-forms such as microbes and eukaryotes and, when conditions were ripe, a new, 'managing', god was created, perhaps by Gaia as implied in the Whale's song. I have not explored this concept in any depth but it does offer an alternative way of using 'evolution' to develop and enhance the functioning of each living creature or plant.

We know that the genetic program for each living being is coded within its genes, using a 'four letter' program, rather than the binary on/off program used by humans in our computers. If a human computer programmer is asked to alter the function of a program to suit changing needs or make it more efficient, he readily does this by altering the code within the program.

Could it be that, if a living creature was recognised by Gaia as needing to change for its survival or enhancement, she could in some way reprogram its genes to achieve this? Humans can, even now, reprogram living creatures and plants by cutting and splicing the double helix of their genetic codes. If such changes initiated by Gaia could only build on what already exists, rather than cut and splice-in the codes from other creatures as humans do, that would explain why it takes a relatively long time for a new species to emerge, although not as long as is implied in the 'survival of the fittest' theory. The following Gaia-initiated concept came out of my subconscious writing mind when I was working on the novel, *Dolphin Song*.

Here is the passage as I wrote it –

> *'I once heard a Great Whale sing,' said Nordstar* [A pilot whale].
> *'Could you understand its song?' FairIsle* [a dolphin] *asked.   'Mostly, but I was overwhelmed by fear of my destiny at the time and did not do justice to the privilege.'*
> *'What did it sing?' asked FairIsle eagerly, as they circled in the darkness.*
> *'It seemed that this whale was the last of her Chapter to be alive and she held knowledge known to no other whale. Knowledge of what she called the Wishful Mixing of Life.'*
> *'Could you understand her meanings?'*

'A little. I had swum away from my constellation [family group] to be on my own and meditate, and this whale was seemingly desperate to tell some other creature of what it was that she alone knew. She sang, and I listened as best I knew how.

'She told me how all creatures pass on their body shapes and their instincts to the next generations as patterns in their seeds.'   'Patterns?' asked FairIsle. 'Patterns like ripples down the edges of kelpweed was how this whale tried to describe it to me. I found it hard to follow. She said that females have one pattern in their seeds and males another pattern in theirs. When the seeds combine at Joy-sharing [mating] it is as though a whirlpool had twisted the kelp-strands together and somehow merged them. The combined ripples direct the making of the new-life which has in it some of each parent.'

'How did she know that?' FairIsle asked.

'She did not say. The intellects of the great whales are far superior to ours. Perhaps it was just speculation – mere fancy.'

'Even so, it is a wonderful idea,' said FairIsle. 'All whalekind should know of that.'

'That was the concern of the Great Whale. But she told me much more.'

'More? Tell me.'

'She said that she believed a female's mind can alter the patterns, but only before the joining of her seed with the male's. If she desires something enough – like being able to swim faster, dive deeper or understand more clearly – and wishes it for the future, then the power of her mind can alter the patterns, but only a little. It takes *many generations of similar desires before the effects are visible.'*

'Only the females can do this?'

'She did not say. Perhaps the males can do the same with their seed.'

'That's extraordinary,' said FairIsle. 'The whale told you all of this?'

'And more that I have forgotten, or did not understand. I hope she has found others of her kind to whom she can pass it on. When knowledge is held by only a few, it is fearfully vulnerable to loss.'

'Humans record things outside of their minds,' broke in Rockall [another dolphin]. 'That's why they have hands.' He slapped his tail on the water, pleased that he knew something the females didn't.

'That's extraordinary,' said FairIsle for the second time.

'There are more mysteries in the Sea and Sky than even dolphins dream of,' said Rockall, slapping the water again.

There is a further implication in the above. Nordstar is saying that the Great Whale told her that creatures, (in this case whales) can change their genetic codes *themselves* by the power of their own minds in wishing to become more 'efficient'.

I am just not experienced enough, nor do I have the time if I am going to publish this book, to follow this idea through and see if it has any validity. However, both the concept of the 'Gaia creating Mana' scenario outlined in the whale's song to the elephant, and what the Great Whale called 'The

Wishful Mixing of Life' came as inspiration when writing, so I can't just suppress these ideas as too fanciful even though I know and accept that many readers will.

Part Two. Chapter Eight.

Summary of Part Two.

Time perhaps to look back on the points we have covered in Part Two.

In Chapter One I invited you to test everything I was suggesting against your own experiences to see if they 'chimed for you'.

In Chapter Two I suggested that God might be a version of the way our bodies and intelligences work, scaled-up to Planet Size and using *our* bodies and intelligences to form a network of senses and a vast Super-Intelligence.

In Chapter Three I developed the Body analogy by inviting you to imagine yourself to be a fingertip nerve cell in your own body to make the point that we do not have to know the 'purpose' to play our part in this planet-based God. We then discussed the role of 'Free Will' in this.

In Chapter Four we tackled the question of whether or not God was 'all mighty' and how we might be inspired to work his will – as well as why we might have been brought up with certain beliefs.

In Chapter Five we discussed Joy and Love and speculated that Divine Energy (Dark Matter) could be the raw material energising these.

In Chapter Six we went on to discuss Truth and Beauty and their relationship to each other, to Joy and Love, and to ourselves.

In Chapter Seven we rather fancifully considered whether Mana God could have been created by a Gaia Goddess and extended this concept using the Whale's song from the book, *God's Elephants*, and the Great Whale's ideas on 'The Wishful Mixing Of life' from *Dolphin Song*.

Here is a challenging statement. *It doesn't matter if I have got any of the foregoing only partially right, or even if I am completely and utterly wrong – if you follow the suggestions in Part Three, you will be happier and the world will be a better place.*

The Ferry Boat

Part Three

Part Three. Chapter One.

Making Contact.

If, having stayed with me this far, you may well believe as I do, that there does exist on Planet Earth a God who is less than all mighty but is interested in the welfare of you and me, you will probably be asking, 'What should I do next for the benefit of God/Mana and myself?'

(A note of explanation – In Part Two I floated the idea of there being both a creative Goddess, *Gaia* and a later creation of hers, *Mana*, who was needed to 'manage' affairs on a developing planet. I admitted to being unable to extend this idea, at least within the time scale I have allowed for publication of *The Ferry Boat*, so have confined the rest of this book to our relationship with God/Mana.)

You may recall from Part One, that I left school before my sixteenth birthday with no clear idea of what I wanted to do with my life. I was the holder of a General Certificate of Education at Ordinary level with just three modest passes though later, when I was in the Royal Air Force and seeking promotion, I did make the effort and gain another four. At no time did I even consider going on to further education and in those days only a small percentage of young people went to university. Now I consider this to have been a benefit to me as my experience of life has been far wider than if I had been channelled into a particular study area or profession.

When I read the books by eminent scientists regarding their theories about God and the origins of the universe, they seem to be hung up on having to offer scientific proof for every statement they make. So much so, that the ordinary seeker of truth is confused and frequently struggles to follow the argument – even to the point where, like me, they abandon the book half-read.

It would appear that all too often in the academic world, there is no room for imaginative speculation in case their peers ridicule their suggestions as happened to Professor Hardy when he proposed the theory of The Aquatic Ape. Such ridicule in Academia can adversely affect the reputations, the status and the prospects of advancement of the proposer. Happily for me, I have no such constraints and, being used to allowing my imagination full range in the writing of my novels, I can cheerfully float out ideas that I cannot justify except by saying that 'they chime with me', or that 'they fit in with my personal experiences of life over the last 73 years.'

When my first lovely baby girl was born, my mother – who was well qualified to do so having had six children of her own– offered the following advice to my wife.

What my mother said was, 'Every woman you know will give you advice on how to look after the baby. They will tell you which books to read, how to feed her, bath her, burp her, change her nappies and what to do if she cries. Ignore all this advice – just do what feels right to you!'

I don't think my mother realised the irony of her suggesting that we should ignore *all* advice and then suggesting some of her own, but she was spot on – 'just do what feels right to you!'

I have tried desperately in this book to avoid saying what one should or must do and most of all I have tried to avoid preaching. I would just suggest that you take my dear mother's advice and 'do what feels right to you!' If any proposals don't chime with you – ignore them!

Firstly, we need to set up a form of communication with God (or Mana if you prefer). If you haven't already done this through an established religious faith, here is what I suggest you do. It is absurdly simple. You do not need to sign on any dotted lines, go through any kind of official ceremony, wear special clothes or behave in a conspicuously different way. Just listen to an inner voice, which is sometimes called your conscience. One expects God's voice to be loud and insistent but often it is not. In one of my wildlife novels, Tembella Grace, a wise old elephant, tells a seeking youngster, *'You expect a roar and you hear a whisper!'*

At first you are unsure that what you hear is in fact the voice of God speaking directly to you but, if you listen carefully, you will find that you are inspired to only do good or right things – never anything that you might subsequently be ashamed of. Inspiration can be at many levels, from just being inspired to smile at a lonely person or sending a gift to a charity, up to devoting your entire life to medical research.

In setting up a line of communication with God, I stated that no special formalities or ceremonies were required. However, after long discussions with a friend whose opinions I value, I agree with her that most of us need some kind of symbolic act when we make significant changes to our lives. Here are three suggestions to help you start your communication.

If you are lucky enough, as I am, to live in the country, go to some quiet place carrying a wooden stick and rest one end on the ground whilst holding the other end with both hands. Think of the stick as plugging you into the ground. Look around you at the wonderful and beautiful plants, birds and animals and say, out loud or just within your head, *'Here I am, God. I'm listening'*.

If you live in a city and can't get to the countryside, or a private enough place in the open air, buy yourself a simple candle, light it, look at the flame, shut out the soulless hassle and bustle of city-life and say, out loud or just within your head, *'Here I am, God. I'm listening.'*

Should you have been brought up to attend church but have found that going through the motions, without a true belief, does not lead to meaningful communication, try going into *any* church and sit there quietly, away from other people. Ideally, reach out and touch a wall or a pillar, sense the generations of spiritual outpourings that have occurred there and say, out loud or just within your head, *'Here I am, God. I'm listening.'*

I quote a beautiful poem by my friend and fellow poet, Barbara Ann Knight –

Flame-spell

I light my candle, pride renouncing, as I bow my head
In silence, try to hear your soul-entrancing word.
A softer light shines through the stained-glass window.
In draughts from open doors the flame is stirred.

The flickering fire-glow soothes and guides my spirit,
One moment out of hastening time is caught
In nets of stillness, softly-breathing bodies round me,
Others gathered, waiting for the peaceful thought.

Just for this once, I stop my chase for worldly honour,
Soft step in wonder where the priests of centuries have trod.
I shed my Self, surrender to the dim-lit quietness
      And 'I am listening, God'.

You may get a response immediately, or you may not. It doesn't matter – you will have registered. Just be alert for a response. Keep your *wish to communicate* in your head and wait to hear what God wants of you. Bear in mind the old elephant's comment, 'You expect a roar and you hear a whisper'. You may get a message that you can easily identify as God's voice or it may just manifest itself in your being inspired to smile at a stranger, offer companionship to a lonely person or carry out random acts of kindness. (I love that phrase.)

Sometime soon after this, you will recognise that you are now actively 'in tune' spiritually with God. If I am right in what I believe, then it is likely that what we see, *God sees*, what we hear, *God hears*, what we experience, *God experiences*. I see this in a positive way, *not* that God is spying on us or using our senses to observe and judge others. Using our senses in this way enables him to know what is going on where *we* are and to decide on how to influence and guide us, and others near us, in the best way to suit his plans.

As God's power is limited, you still retain what is known as 'Free Will', which is the licence to do what you like, subject to the laws of the land where you live.

I hope that you are, or will be, convinced that *your* life is going to be much more fulfilled if you can live it in a way that fits in with God's (undisclosed) plans for the future of this planet. It is not our right to know these plans – we just have to accept that what he would like us to do is best for us all.

This is a partnership of mutual benefit. One of God's most important concerns must be for the future health and survival of the planet which is his 'home', just as one of *our* most important concerns is for the health and survival of our own bodies which are 'home' to our intelligence. Hence, the more people who cooperate in fulfilling his plan, the better it will be for all of us who have the privilege of living for a time on this wonderful planet.

In the chapter on Joy and Love in Part Two, we discussed the possibility that the Love we create from experiencing Joy not only benefits us and raises our experience of life to a higher level, but that it is this Love which *powers* God. It follows therefore, that we should now be seeking even more Joy and from it creating even more Love.

How different this attitude is to those that load us with guilt and suggest that enjoying life to the full is sinful and unworthy of a 'true believer'. I am sure that God wants us to enjoy all that this wonderful planet has to offer, provided that it is not at the expense of others.

Part Three. Chapter Two

Heaven, Hell and Immortality.

Several of the established faiths make great play on the existence of a Heaven, where those of us who had kept the commandments of that faith will live for eternity in a state of bliss, and of a Hell where the rest of us would burn in torment until the end of time.

Someone once said, 'The day I lost my fear of Hell, I lost my hope of Heaven'. I thought, at the time I first heard this, that it seemed a good deal! Hell, as described in Christian literature and art, especially of the Middle Ages, is so horrible that, to give up one's hope of Heaven would be a worthwhile sacrifice if it could take away all fear of spending Eternity in everlasting torment.

Even in my most naive state of mind, I could not believe that a loving God could condemn even the worst-behaving human to such an ordeal. However, I was rather more ready to accept a heavenly paradise where one's soul could exist in an approximately human form and be reunited there with the loved ones who had died before you had. But this concept, appealing though it was, had always struck me as mere wishful thinking. One major factor in doubting the existence of a heaven was where in the Universe, or beyond, could such a place exist?

By bringing our God back down to Earth-size, the question becomes even more impossible to answer. Frankly, I do not believe in the existence of either a dreadful Hell or a wonderful Heaven. I believe that both were part of the propaganda inflicted on our forebears by arrogant men who wished to control subjects or congregations, for purposes of their own. They used the threatening stick – 'Know your place! Do what I tell you or you will be doomed to suffer for the whole of Eternity!' – and the tempting carrot – 'But if you do comply, I can promise you everlasting joy and happiness.' What incredible and sickening manipulation, especially when done in the name of a loving God!

Yet most thinking people have a yearning for some sort of immortality. Those of us fortunate enough to have children (I have three) and grandchildren (I have three of these as well and one recently born great-grandchild,) can see a kind of immortality through them. What we now call our genes will carry a part of ourselves through to future generations, although *our* contribution is diluted by 50% each time. (Only $1/8^{th}$ of the genes of my great-grandchild are mine and only $1/16^{th}$ in the next generation.)

If we are writers, artists, poets, composers of music, or creators of other lasting works, this too gives us a form of immortality. Shakespeare and Beethoven live on to this day and will probably do so for a very long time'

Nobody is dead
Whilst others enjoy their work –
And are influenced.

But the foregoing forms of immortality are not in any way a substitute for a heavenly paradise.

Earlier, I suggested that our Earth-sized God was a scaled-up version of our own bodies and intelligences, who used our bodies, brains and sensory organs to function as a Being which is both vastly bigger and more intelligent

100

than ourselves but which needs *us* to exist at all. I find this concept both exciting and humbling. What a privilege to be a vital part of this Being and what a responsibility as well! If we, during our lifetimes, serve God as best we can, we are a part of his Being in the same way as the cells of our bodies and brains are a part of us.

We also learned how our cells live for a much shorter time than we do and, as each cell dies, it is replaced by another which takes over the function of the dead cell. This means that, after a time, our entire body and brain has been replaced – yet we appear to be the same as before. We function in the same way, other people still recognise us and, most amazingly, we still have the same memories. In some way, the dying brain cells have handed on the memories held by the group of cells of which they were a part, to their replacements. One could therefore say that these cells, even though they have died individually, live on as long as we do.

Let's scale this concept up to God size. If I have played a cell-like role in God's Being and have helped develop God's knowledge and intelligence, and then I die as an individual human, does my intelligence (or soul) not live on in God in the same way as the contents of my defunct brain cells (my intelligence) live on in me until I die? If so, *that* is what I would call immortality!

Until we are able to recognise this important point, many of us fear the apparent loss of personal identity implicit in our deaths. Here is a story to illustrate that this need not be so –

When I was about sixty years old, I joined a club whose nearest branch was over fifty miles away. Each fortnight I would drive to the club and enjoy an evening with kindred spirits. After a while, I felt that I should play some active part in the running of the club but lived too far away for it to be sensible to drive such a long way to attend the brief committee meetings. As I was self-employed and did not have to work fixed hours, I took on the role of preparing the room beforehand. I would set out the chairs, fetch equipment for the meeting and greet the members and guests as they arrived and then clear away afterwards. This was a fairly menial but important role.

I was surprised therefore when I was invited to become president of that branch without serving in any of the more senior roles. I took the role on as I had become concerned that standards had been falling and consequently many members did not bother to attend. Gently, during my year in office, I encouraged better punctuality, more appropriate dress and positive encouragement for new members.

When the time came to hand over the presidency, the club was undoubtedly in better shape, stronger, more vibrant and more enjoyable for all members. Sometime later, due to ill health, I had to give up attending. I personally missed the meetings very much but took comfort in the knowledge that the club itself (far more important than me) was continuing in strong form and does so to this day.

Now, when I occasionally meet members, they kindly tell me that I was much missed and that, had I not made my contribution that year, the club may have faded away. (I tell this story, not to pat myself on the back for being a good president but to show how one's contribution to *anything* can have a lasting effect.)

If I am right in my interpretation of God/Mana as a Being composed of the intelligences of all people who are 'signed in' as members of the Planet Earth God Club, then each of us has an input to make. Each of us can contribute to the effective running of this very special club and, when we die, the Club (God/Mana) continues without us. However, *we are still there* in its continuation, due to our support and influence during our membership. Note that this has not been a one-sided effort. Whilst we have been making our contribution, we have been enjoying all the benefits of membership such as loving and being loved, and being able to appreciate the good things happening around us.

Death, however much we would like to defer it, is not a sudden end, leaving nothing of value, but a fading out of ourselves whilst leaving our influences to support a much larger and more important Being (God) to continue, stronger and more vibrant, due to our modest input.

Throughout history people have searched for an answer to this 'what happens to *me* after I die' question. God seems remarkably reticent to give a clear answer to that question, so I have to leave it there. However I am totally convinced that God has no future Hell waiting for us. I believe that we either exist after death in some continuing (heavenly) way – and are joyfully aware of it then – or as a lasting influence, even if we have no awareness of this after we have died.   Should I be wrong, we just will not be aware at all. On this basis, none of us need have any fear about dying.

Part Three. Chapter Three

God – The Father.

The concept of God as a loving father is deeply embedded in the Christian Faith. Even the prayer taught by Jesus of Nazareth starts, 'Our Father...'

As a father myself, I feel this is an accurate parallel to the relationship between God and ourselves. A father is (or should be), immensely supportive of his children, helping them in every way he can and readily forgiving them when they do not live up to his desired standards. He will protect them to the best of his ability, guide and teach them in what they need to do and how to behave and, even if they disappoint in some areas, he will still love them and be proud of their achievements.

In return, a loving son or daughter will respect their father and be ready to put themselves out to assist him in whatever *he* is trying to achieve, even if they don't fully understand his motives at the time. If one keeps this father/son or father/daughter parallel as an ideal in your relationship with God, I believe that you will find it easy to know how to act.

Just as a father will try to provide what their children require, so too will God try to provide what you require (or think that you require) and this brings us back to Synchronicity. If a child wants something but does not make its needs known, especially in a large family, it is likely that the father won't provide it – not because he can't or won't but because he is unaware of the need or desire. Remember that a fundamental part of this understanding of God is that he is not 'all mighty'! It is therefore up to us to let him know our needs and desires.

In Part One I described in considerable detail several synchronistic events that I had experienced on my spiritual journey. I cannot overemphasise the importance of these in convincing me of the existence of a God who was prepared to communicate with me, help and guide me.

My dictionary offers this definition of *synchronicity* – 'an apparently meaningful coincidence in time of two or more similar or identical events that are causually unrelated.' You may recall that I defined synchronicity in earlier chapters as:-

When you have set yourself on a benign path, the most amazing things happen to help you along that path – but you must be receptive enough to recognise what is being provided.

When we were children, at Christmas many of us made lists addressed to Santa Claus and sent them (via our parents) to his home at the North Pole. Our parents, loving us as they did, tried to ensure that we received at least the presents at the top of the list. Early in this book I described the response to my *wish* for a Volvo Estate car and later to my *wish* to find a way for my dolphin character to communicate with humans in an original way. These wishes, you may recall, were answered by other people being inspired, apparently without their knowledge, to help me.

On the occasion of my needing a special activity for my fictitious elephants (which turned out to be making rain), I felt I had been shown this by God directly, but there might have been some unseen activity, on a spiritual level, by the bushmen living in the area. I don't know – and I don't need to know. It happened and I am content with that.

If you still don't believe this can happen for you I would just urge you to give it a try, within these simple guide lines:-

1. Only ask for something that is possible. For example, if you fancy flying like a bird, it is no good asking to grow feathers and wings but, if you ask to be able to 'experience flight without the intrusive noise of an engine', you may be surprised how soon you will find yourself in a glider or launching yourself off a hillside under a paragliding wing.

    Cynics will say, 'Once you had thought that *this* is what you wanted to do more than anything else, *you* went and organised it!' Yes, maybe *you* did – but it worked. Remember the saying, 'God helps those who help themselves'.

    If your house is repossessed, as mine once was, it is no good asking for a new, mortgage-free house, ask instead for a pleasant home to live in whilst you rebuild you life, and recognise that your wish has been granted when someone offers a suitable one for you to rent. It may not be exactly what you had in mind but be prepared to consider it but, if it doesn't 'click', reject it and keep that wish at the top of your list.

2. Only ask for something you *need* or *want very much*. If we are going to ask God for something we

should be serious about it – anything less I would rate as an insult!

3. Keep your list short. I would suggest that three items at a time is the absolute maximum. One at a time would be better.

4. Don't ask repeatedly for the same item, but do keep focused on watching for your wish to be satisfied.

5. When your wish *is* granted, acknowledge receipt. You don't need to send a 'thank you letter'; a simple, sincerely-expressed thought will do.

Why should God be so ready to grant your wishes? Why did your parents try their very best to get you the presents on your wish-list to Santa Claus? Because they loved you. God loves you! And needs you, too.

I was recently lent a book written by a German woman, Barbel Mohr. Her book is called *The Cosmic Ordering Service* and in it she describes how one can 'order up' from what she calls *The Cosmos,* whatever you require. She uses this word *Cosmos* to describe 'the world as an ordered system' rather than the 'Universe', which is perhaps the more usual meaning of cosmos for most of us. She describes much the same system as the one that produced my Volvo car but her approach seems rather flippant to me. She writes about 'ordering up' all sorts of things, including desirable boyfriends who must conform to a wish-list of attributes such as being against alcohol, being a vegetarian, being a non-smoker and knowing T'ai Chi. Barbel Mohr is positive that *all* her orders are fulfilled, even if she has decided in the meantime that she no longer wants whatever it was she had ordered. I am uncomfortable about this approach and feel that, if she is right about this power, it should be used more sparingly and more thoughtfully.

One point she does make with which I do agree, is that all requests should be *positive*. I quote Barbel, "Phrase every order in a positive way! Words like 'not' and 'no' are disadvantageous. For example, you wouldn't call up Sears [a mail-order company] to tell them: 'I don't want to order a green table cloth.' Order that which you would like to have, or have happen, instead. If you would like to 'cancel' a disease, you have to order *health* for the respective body part."

She points out that one must be prepared for the order to be delivered in a form somewhat different to what *you* thought you had ordered.

Here is a story that you may have heard before which illustrates in an amusing way, how one can fail to recognise when one's request has been acted upon.

*A man, who was a strong swimmer, found himself being swept out to sea in a powerful current. Unable to swim back to the shore, he prayed fervently to God to save him and he received an assurance from above that all would be well – God would definitely save him. Soon afterwards, a lifeboat, called out by an alert coastguard, came to rescue him. 'I don't need you,' he told the crew, '****God*** is going to save me.' The lifeboat turned back to base and the man, tiring now, saw a helicopter hovering above him and a lifting-strop being lowered. He waved the helicopter away – he didn't need it – ****God*** had promised to save him!*

Eventually he was so exhausted that he drowned. Arriving at the Pearly Gates, tired out and dripping wet, he complained to Saint Peter that God had promised to save him and had not done so.

'Whose fault is that?' replied Saint Peter. 'He sent a lifeboat and a helicopter – What more did you want Him to do?'

I earlier related a few of my personal synchronistic experiences such as the Volvo car, being inspired to get on the minibus in Ireland and learn about Ogham writing, the baobab talk on the radio and the most exciting one of all, when I made rain fall in the Kalahari Desert. Another, which I have not mentioned before, concerned a house move about five years ago.

Following the serious loss of income I suffered during the time when I was involved with the Water Filter business, I was unable to maintain my mortgage payments and my wife and I had to move into rented accommodation. Here we lived for thirteen years during which I wrote and published my novel, *Dolphin Song*. Then, with little warning, my landlord gave me notice to leave because he was selling the house. As the lovely meadow across the road had just become a building site, I was not too reluctant to go and moved to a house about twenty miles away on a six-month let. Neither my wife nor I were happy there, we had both developed heart problems and I missed being near the mountains far more than I had expected. After about four months, I was beginning to think it was time to be finding another home and one Saturday morning, on my daily walk, I paused by a gate from where I had a distant view of my beloved mountains. Unaware that I was placing what Barbel Mohr would call a 'Cosmic Order', I found I was telling myself (and God) how much I wanted to be nearer those mountains. Two minutes later, I was striding back to the house where I got into my car and drove directly to Abergavenny, my old home-town, which sits in a beautiful river valley with my favourite mountains on either side. The first letting agent I tried had no suitable properties to rent (I had specified to him a cottage in the country) but the second agent asked if I would consider a ground floor flat on the outskirts of town. 'No way,' I told him. 'I can't see me living in a flat – nor in town!'

He persisted. 'It's a rather special flat! It's in a Victorian house in an acre of garden with a stream running through it, the rooms are big and the Brecon Beacons National Park boundary is just across the lane behind it.' He named a house that I had driven past many hundreds of times. At the time this was happening to me, I had no concept that he might have been *inspired* to ignore my stated specification – now I am convinced he had been.

Within two hours I had looked at the flat from the outside, collected my wife, the two of us had been shown round, and I had paid my deposit. It was here I wrote *God's Elephants* and it is here I am now, writing this.

It was here too that I had the chance to renovate the wonderful old greenhouse just when I needed such a project. I am very happy and settled and have no desire to move again. Was this a Cosmic Order satisfactorily delivered? Synchronicity in action? I think so now.

(I don't like the 'Cosmic' title and prefer to call it quite simply a 'Wish-List'. One of my favourite sayings is, 'If you're feeling listless – make a list'.)

On a more day-to-day level, my eldest daughter tells me that, before I told her about Synchronicity, Cosmic Ordering and Targeting, she had always pleaded with 'an unknown force' to make a parking space available for her when she was driving into town. Just as she arrived where she wanted to park, a car would pull out and leave a space for her. Was this coincidence, as many would argue, or was her *unknown force* (God?) hearing her request?

Although I have put my rainmaking experience into a 'synchronistic' category, it is somewhat different to the others. Most such experiences require another human to be an agent in making what you need happen for you. In the Ogham writing event the *bus driver* arrived at just the right moment; with the Volvo incident the *salesman* found a way for me to buy; in finding my current home, the *estate agent* was not put off by my negative response to 'a flat in town'. Were *they* inspired by God/Mana/The Cosmos to act in a way that satisfied my desires? Were the *other drivers* inspired to complete their business in town and drive away just as my daughter was on the way? Some would call all of these mere coincidences but I would, at the very least, call them Super-coincidences!

What makes me exclude the rain-making from the more usual Super-coincidences, is that no other humans were involved. This was an example of God himself satisfying my needs for a special elephant skill for my novel. I feel really privileged to have had that experience and it has helped to convince me that I have indeed *set myself on a benign and worthwhile path.*

Many people pray and prayer is something I had always been sceptical about. Until I came to the conclusion that (our) God was confined to this planet, the idea that a 'bigger than the Universe' God would or could be influenced by our requests, was absurd to me. I was also scathing about people who prayed for help when in danger – but not at other times. In my novel *Dolphin Song*, when the vessel she is on is being battered by a storm at sea, Helga recalls her Uncle Roi saying, *'There are no atheists on a sinking ship!'*

However, could it be that Targeting, Synchronicity and Cosmic Ordering are just other names for praying and prayer? Each is a request for help or attention of some kind, although prayers of *Praise* seem futile to me, as do hymns consisting of the constant *praising* of God. The need or desire to be praised seems unworthy for a being as wonderful as a real God must be. My least favourite word is 'Hallelujah'.

I was taught by the nuns in my primary school that, to pray properly, one had to get down on one's knees, close one's eyes and put one's hands together. Now I find that any prayers or wishes I make are as likely to be answered if I just lie in bed, think positively and formulate my needs clearly.

If we come back to the 'God as a father' analogy, I would not expect my children to be constantly praising or flattering me however much I was able to help them with their ambitions – but I would like to be told what they would like me to do to help them to achieve their needs.

Some people, especially Roman Catholics, pray to Mary, the mother of Jesus, to Jesus himself, or to one of a great number of saints who they believe specialise in providing answers to their current needs. Without ever consciously deciding that I should, I direct my requests to, 'Dear God,' and that seems right to me but I don't believe that any form is wrong, as long as it is sincere and worthy.

I also believe that one should be sparing in one's requests. The term 'God-botherer' describes someone who is constantly praying for this and that or telling God how great he (God) is – which I am sure he already knows! Surely their time would be better spent in helping their own wishes to come true (remember – God helps those who help themselves) or in watching for the answer to their most important prayer – which may come in a form they are not expecting. It would be sad if the response to a vital request were missed because of a failure to recognise it when it appeared.

When I sent out drafts of this books to friends and relatives to garner their views before publication, one friend told me of an instance which she felt was totally in line with *my* synchronistic experiences. She often walked by the local river but had never seen a kingfisher there. One day she felt a strong spiritual need to see one and sat on her usual riverside seat, wishing one would appear. Within minutes a kingfisher perched on a branch nearby and sat there for several minutes observing her in the same way as she was observing it. When it finally flew away she felt that it had been sent especially for her.

I have noticed on my walks in the mountains, that to make a red kite appear I have to think positively about seeing one. These then do become Red Kite Days for me.

As I wrote this, I remembered another apparently synchronistic experience that I had recorded elsewhere. Here is what I had written :-

I visited the Faroe Islands twice when I was writing Dolphin Song, once before starting the book and again when it was drafted so that I could check for accuracy.

On the first visit, I travelled by sea from Aberdeen, a twenty-four hour trip through cold, grey seas. I had not booked anywhere to stay and when I arrived, I walked into Torshavn town and found a 'cheapy' B. and B. I was shown to a twin-bedded room and unpacked. Soon after, the owner came and said that there had been a mistake and the room was not available.

It seemed that another passenger, a young American man, had telephoned from the docks and booked the room. When I arrived the owner had thought that I was him. However, I and the American (Steve) agreed that we had no objection to sharing and it turned out well, as we travelled the islands together, visiting the museum, the Viking Cathedral and the preserved farm-house which was the basis of Helga's house in Dolphin Song.

For some reason I can't recall, my credit card was not accepted by the Torshavn bank, leaving me short of cash and Steve readily lent me money, to be repaid when I got home.

On the return journey, by an equally cold and grey sea, Steve and I were sitting where we could see the water ahead of the ship when Steve said that he'd never seen a dolphin.

I recalled reading that the inhabitants of an island in the Pacific could 'call up' dolphins and I said, on a whim, 'I'll call one up for you.'

Hardly had I said this than a dolphin leapt out of the water about a hundred yards ahead of us. I had not seen any other dolphins on the journey to the Faroes, none whilst I was there and we didn't see any more on the rest of the journey back to Aberdeen.

Had I called it up?

Once again, it is easy to dismiss this as a mere coincidence but, when these sort of happenings occur often, it seems reasonable to me to look for other causes. The essence of this book is that I, and other people I talk with, have all had experiences well beyond mere coincidence.

The friend who told me about her kingfisher also related how, whenever one of her pet cats had died, a stray kitten would turn up within a few days and spend the rest of its life well-fed and well-loved.

If God/Mana can find a human near enough to you and inspire them to provide for your declared wishes, it is probably simple for him to find a bird or animal to appear on cue to give you joy – especially if it is a hungry kitten.

When writing about the kingfisher, I was reminded that I have never been able to finish a poem I started composing many years ago in which I compared 'happiness' to a kingfisher. Unlike my friend's kingfisher, I have always found that any kingfishers that I have seen, flash past with a shrill call and just a glimpse of blue and orange.

One of my Kernels of Truth states

Rainbows, kingfishers
And happiness – don't stay long
Each a fleeting joy.

I was never able to get beyond the first two verses and the last line of the longer poem, which reads

'The fleeting kingfisher of happiness.'

In this line, and in the Kernel, the essence of the thought is the *fleeting* nature of happiness.

You may have noticed that I have seldom used 'happiness' as a life-goal in this book whereas I have often used the words 'joy' and 'joyful'.

In the same way that the word 'almighty' has become linked to that of 'god' in many religions, so the word 'happiness' has become a key life-goal in many western cultures. This has been led by the lines in the American Declaration of Independence –

'We hold these truths to be self-evident, that all men are created equal, that they are endowed by their Creator with certain unalienable Rights, that among these are Life, Liberty and the pursuit of Happiness.'

We all experience some 'happy' events in our lives but these are usually short lived and generally happen un-expectedly. As a goal we would be better off aiming for

Joy, which lasts long enough to create Love and which, when really long-lasting, becomes Contentment.

Whilst on this topic, should one say 'thank you' when a request is granted? I believe that God does not require thanks any more than he needs praise, but I do think that a grateful 'thank you' never comes amiss, be it to God, to your own father or to any other person who has helped you in some way.

Finally, should we confess our 'sins' and ask for forgiveness? I think not – although this is contrary to traditional Christian teaching. If we are in tune with God he will know when we have done something of which we are ashamed. I would not expect my children to tell me when they had done something wrong. I am not their judge and would continue to love them and help them anyway. However, if they needed my help to get out of a mess their wrongdoing had got them into, I would expect them to ask for my help, which I would give unstintingly. I would trust God/Mana to do the same for us.

Part Three. Chapter Four

Fear and Pain.

I was once told that the opposite of love is fear, which did not chime with me as I knew that the opposite of love is defined as 'hate'. However, my mind just wouldn't let go of this – there was something more here that I needed to explore.

Another saying came to mind, 'When Poverty comes in the door, Love flies out the window'. Modify this slightly to, 'When Fear comes in the door, Love flies out the window,' and the relationship between love and fear becomes more apparent.

Fear is a horrible emotion which can paralyse people into a state of panic, or almost as bad – inaction. There is certainly little room for Joy and Love when Fear is in the room.

I am lucky in that I have only been in fear of my life once, when the R.A.F. rescue team of which I was a member was trapped on an unstable cliff-face whilst on a training exercise in Kenya in 1963. Even though it was almost fifty years ago and we all got off safely, I still shudder when I remember having to overcome a paralysing fear and find a way to firmer ground.

There have, of course, been many lesser incidents before and after that where I experienced fear and had to do something about it. You may recall that I married early, in fact the first wedding I ever went to was my own! I am sure that many bridegrooms and brides have sleepless nights prior to their weddings, wondering if they are doing the right thing – I certainly did. Each time I thought of the wedding and the commitment I was about to make, a huge black cloud rolled into my mind blanking out all logical thought. As the wedding day drew nearer, I had to do something about this and I decided to force myself to face up to my fears. I lay in bed, sweating, and asked myself , 'What are you afraid of? Out with it!' The cloud rolled away and the reply came, 'You are afraid that you don't love her as much as you should if you are going to spend the rest of your lives together'.

I searched my feelings to see if this was true and discovered that it wasn't – I loved my fiancée deeply. I had no doubts at all about my love. The clouds were gone, the marriage went ahead and, fifty-three years later, I can look back with no regrets.

I tell this story as it illustrates an important way to tackle fear. Face up to it! Ask yourself, 'What is the worst possible outcome? Can I cope with that if it happens?' Often the answer is an easy 'yes' and the fear disappears.

Another is to have a Plan B. Plan A is doing what you are doing anyway, but devise a Plan B in case it doesn't work out. Fear comes when you don't have a Plan B. Sometimes your Plan B will seem better than your Plan A. If so, abandon Plan A and go straight to Plan B.

Of course, here I am not talking about such fears as a fear of violence from a bully or from a dangerous partner. These are often beyond one's own ability to deal with. If you find yourself in this sort of situation, seek help at once – putting it off will only make it worse. Ask for help from family or friends or, if these are absent, from a priest or a charity worker who has shown themselves to be ready to 'serve' voluntarily. Ask God/Mana for guidance. But most importantly – get away somehow to a place of safety. Here you can reduce your fears, recover your composure and, with help, start anew.

Another kind of Fear is a fear of loss – loss of a loved one, loss of your job, loss of your home, loss of your reputation – serious losses that really hurt. Life, especially now, will almost certainly involve you in one or more of these. I have suffered many such losses and, after the event, they do not seem to have been as bad as I had feared beforehand. A favourite Kernel of Truth is

True security
Comes from the acceptance of
Insecurity.

Easy to say, I know, but true.

All the time, in all situations, remember God/Mana is available in his role of a loving father. Speak to him, express your fears, ask for help and then listen for guidance.

Pain evolved as a way of letting our brains know that some part of our bodies had been hurt so that the brain could instruct some other part to take action to reduce or eliminate this danger. For example, if I as a primitive being, touched a burning stick, the pain I felt would make me immediately pull my hand away. If the skin had been damaged, a different sort of pain would warn me to avoid using that hand until the skin had healed.

If I had eaten something mildly poisonous, the pain in my stomach would warn me not to eat it again. If I was severely damaged, or fatally poisoned, the pain would be much worse and I would probably die and I would be in severe pain until that happened.

In more modern times however, doctors would most likely save my life but, until a hundred and fifty or so years ago, I would have continued in severe pain until I was cured or I died. Then painkillers were developed, often from what we would now consider to be dangerous drugs. Until then, I can imagine the person afflicted, and their family, wondering how a loving and almighty God could allow such suffering to exist. Another saying from that time: 'What can't be cured must be endured'.

I particularly dislike the belief, current then, that 'suffering is good for the soul'. I would submit that it was because God/Mana, not being all mighty, was unable to do anything about this but that he hated it as much as those who were suffering. What he *was* able to do was to inspire generations of doctors and scientists to develop a range of medicines and treatments to alleviate or even eliminate the pain.

My father believed that he could substantially reduce pain by the power of thought – 'saying' to the part that was hurting, 'I've got the message. You don't need to keep reminding me to be careful.' However, after he had had a replacement hip-joint and was being driven some long distance home from the hospital, he admitted that it didn't always work. I have tried this and it can work but only for a short time.

If you have a minor pain and ask God/Mana/the Cosmos to reduce it or take it away, this wish can often be granted, but the ready availability of modern painkillers is also part of the benevolent way God can help us. I am sure that doctors and scientists are being inspired to develop even more effective painkillers.

I have not included the very real emotional pains experienced by some unfortunate people. These are nearer to the *fears* discussed in the first part of this chapter and might be resolved in similar ways.

Part Three. Chapter Five

Service.

To most younger people today, the word 'service' either suggests military service by members of the armed forces or the concept of being 'in service', as exemplified by the domestic servants of a past age. The essence being that you undertake dangerous or demeaning actions because you have to, or are ordered to. I see it as being much wider than that. To me 'service' is *taking personal action to ensure that the right and necessary things get done.* In military service, the servicemen and servicewomen do their utmost to carry out the tasks allotted to them even if they are not fully in the know about the reasons for doing them. In domestic service the cooks, butlers, footmen and chambermaids were mostly proud to be 'of service' to their employer, especially if they did a good job and felt that they were appreciated. (And they were paid for it, of course.)

One might readily recognise that fire-fighters, the police and coastguards provide a service but so too do doctors, nurses, vets, bin-men, bus-drivers and many others in similar jobs and professions. These services are all in fact 'paid-for' employment. Outside of these, are the services provided by Mountain Rescue teams, the crews of lifeboats, the voluntary wardens of National Parks, the street collectors for charities and so many more.

Why do the latter group undertake time-consuming and sometimes dangerous tasks without pay and frequently without their efforts receiving adequate recognition? The answer is that their actions ensure that *the right and necessary things get done.* So I am not alone in my understanding of 'service'. But what was it that started them off in the first place when the majority of other people do nothing beyond what they have to, or what they are paid to do? Could it be that they have been *inspired* to do so? The answer has to be 'yes', even if they were unaware that this inspiration may have come from God/Mana.

In the previous chapter, we discussed how to let God know what we wished for. Now I would like to suggest what we offer in return. If you have made a connection with God/Mana as proposed earlier, you might find that God asks something from you which might well come in the shape of a desire to 'be of service'. This might not come in the form of an invitation to coach young people in football or to collect money for charity – but for some task for which *you* are especially qualified. Neither does it imply that you will suffer whilst you are doing the task(s). In fact, it is likely that you will get a great deal of personal joy and satisfaction.

Here is a personal experience to illustrate this. Some years after I left the Royal Air Force, I was approached by the then Chief Warden of the Monmouthshire section of the Brecon Beacons National Park, a remarkable man named Wilf Davies, who lived near the head of a valley in the Black Mountains. I had recently built a dry-stone wall on the boundary of the cottage I was living in at the time, using a skill I had acquired as a teenager on the farm. Wilf had noticed this and enrolled me as a part-time Assistant Warden (unpaid). He had a wonderful way of getting other people to help him achieve his aims of improving the National Park for the benefit of visitors and those who lived there. When a stone wall needed repair or rebuilding, Wilf would ring me up, or come and visit me, and say something along the lines of, "There's a bit of a wall near Llanthony Abbey that has collapsed. Do you think you could spare half a day or so to help me rebuild it? It needs doing very well and I thought of you." How could one refuse a request put like that?

As a consequence, I would cheerfully spend a weekend (whatever happened to the 'half a day'?) working alongside Wilf to rebuild that wall. The exercise was good for me, the setting was magnificent, the chance to refresh my skills was welcome and Wilf's company (sharing a love of the poet, Robert Service's verse by quoting it to each other as we worked) was most enjoyable. Even now, when I see that section of wall we built, I get pleasure from the memories and a pride in the work we did together.

I am now going to offer a new analogy that I call the 'Planet Earth plc.' analogy. Picture this lovely planet of ours as a vibrant company with God/Mana as its C.E.O. (Chief Executive Officer). The C.E.O. has a clear vision of what his company is all about but he has to use other directors, managers and employees to do the actual work to make this happen.

God, as C.E.O. of Planet Earth plc., knows what he wishes to achieve – which must include the continuation of this planet as a viable place for life to exist. He may well have other aims of which we are ignorant but, as I have stated before, these are his concern, not ours.

A C.E.O. has to appoint the right people to undertake the roles and tasks necessary for the effective operation of his company. He will, all the time, be looking for different talents and skills in employees at all levels in the company so that, when a job needs doing or a role needs filling, he can appoint the person most likely to do it satisfactorily.

Let's try this out in a fictitious engineering company. A new employee (Joe) starts work as a stock clerk in the Company Stores. Joe works hard and does his job well. When a vacancy occurs for a stock controller, the C.E.O. (or someone acting for him), who has noticed Joe's efforts, appoints him to the role, which is naturally more demanding. Joe continues to do well and, after a time a manager's position is soon to become vacant. The C.E.O. considers Joe for this position but is not sure how he will perform under the pressures of a manager's job. It is quite likely (and sensible) for Joe to be given temporary extra, difficult and challenging jobs to see if he is up to it. If he succeeds, he is likely to be given the job, if not, he stays where he is and may not even know he had been considered.

Could it be that when we encounter difficult and challenging times in our lives, that God is testing our suitability for a greater role in his plans? If God/Mana has chosen me to write this book to help other people to communicate with him, and to enjoy his largesse and serve his will, he has certainly tested me!

Part Three. Chapter Six

The Three Bs.

In Jewish and Christian religions, the basic rules are contained in the Ten Commandments, which I had to learn as a child. Just in case you don't know them, or don't remember them fully, here they are (in a truncated form):-

1. You shall not worship any other God.
2. You shall not make a graven image.
3. You shall not take the name of God in vain.
4. You shall not break the Sabbath.
5. You shall not dishonour your parents.
6. You shall not murder.
7. You shall not commit adultery.
8. You shall not steal.
9. You shall not commit perjury.
10. You shall not covert things that don't belong to you.

When I read these again after so long, I am struck by two things. Firstly they are all negative – 'You shall not...' 'You shall not...' – and secondly, I ask myself how many young people today would really understand the first four?

One should remember that these commandments were supposedly given by God to Moses when he was leading a band of troublesome ex-slaves out of Egypt to find 'The Promised Land'. In the context of the time – several thousand years ago – and the place – a barren desert - these were probably very relevant, but are they still as relevant in 21st Century Society? I submit that there is a need for a set of new, but simple and *positive,* rules now.

When writing my novel *God's Elephants* I introduced an historical character named Tembo Jay who played the same role in relation to elephants 2000 years ago, as Jesus of Nazareth played for humans. Both Jesus and Tembo Jay taught that gentleness and a care and love for others was a better way to live than being concerned only with one's personal needs.

When I was writing about Tembo Jay, I envisaged that he had condensed this philosophy into a song that had 'got lost' sometime in the intervening years, even though the elephants still lived by the tenets of this. I had not composed the song in advance and I spent a lot of time and effort working out just how Tembo Jay's teachings could be condensed into a simple message.

When I reached the place in the story where the Lost Song was found, I was surprised to find the whole song was complete in my mind and all I had to do was write it down. Here is the passage from the book [Rafiki, Kidogo and M'zee are all elephant characters].

Rafiki paused on the edge of the fire-pit, looked down into it and moved his trunk to hold the tusk [of the long-dead Tembo Jay] more securely. Once more the wet ivory touched against his own single tusk. This time, he and all the other tembos [elephants] heard the voice. It was singing –

'Be kind, be gentle, and be fair
Find Joy and turn it into Love
Create enough for all to share.
When life is more than you can bear
Seek Joy and turn it into Love
Be kind, be gentle, and be fair.

When others mock – brace up and dare
They do not know the Joy of Love
Create enough for all to share.
Don't be afraid – show that you care
Teach how to turn that Joy to Love
Be kind, be gentle, and be fair.

If no one listens – don't despair
Just practise turning Joy to Love
Create enough for all to share.
The simple truth will soon be clear
That all we need is Joy and Love
Create enough for all to share
Be kind, be gentle, and be fair.'

Into the utter stillness and sense of wellbeing that had filled the Mount, Kidogo eventually spoke in a voice all the tembos could hear.

'Remember that song,' she said. 'And now—' She raised her trunk, and Rafiki let the second huge tusk slide over the edge of the pit.

In the silence that followed, M'zee lumbered forward.

'I come,' he said in a hollow voice. 'I come gladly, for I have heard the lost Song of Tembo Jay ...'

Here was the simple message for the elephants – *'Be kind, be gentle and be fair'* and it is this simple maxim that I propose we all adopt to test our actions against.

I call these **The Three B**s – **B**e Kind, **B**e Gentle and **B**e Fair. If one was to apply these to whatever one was doing in life, one wouldn't need stern 'commandments'. I tried long and hard to find a name for these three B's similar to 'The Ten Commandments' but reflecting their real role in one's life. The obvious name was 'The Three Commandments' or 'The Three New Commandments' but both these names sounded harsh and inappropriate. 'Concepts' or 'precepts' did not fully explain what they implied either. 'Guide lines' seemed better, or 'Pointers', but these too did not fit properly. I finally decided that they were just 'Rules', such as one has in games. To play any game well, one abides by the rules but one is not executed or severely punished if you occasionally break a 'rule'.

When faced with a major, or even a minor decision, as to whether or not to take a certain action, test it against the Three Bs rule. Is the proposed action Kind, Gentle and Fair? If 'yes' then go ahead – if 'no', then don't. How delightfully simple!

Another joy of the above is that everybody knows the meanings of the words, 'kind', 'gentle' and 'fair'. It would be hard for even the most crafty lawyer to argue against what everybody would perceive as the real meaning of these words. But this is not about legal definitions and Courts of Law – this is about how we conduct our day to day lives.

Part Three. Chapter Seven.

In Conclusion.

If, after reading this far, you are as convinced as I am that there is a living and loving God here on Planet Earth, I am sure that you will want to establish a permanent relationship with him. Let's remind ourselves how simple it is.

No fancy ceremonies, no vows of everlasting faithfulness, no dressing up, no cash to pay out – just find a quiet time and place and say, "Here I am, God. I'm listening.' Don't expect an immediate answer – such as I received near the Humpy Bog – because it doesn't always happen that way. Also remember what the wise old elephant, Tembella Grace, told the young Temba Kidogo in *God's Elephants*, 'You expect a roar and you hear a whisper'. The reply will sometimes be so quiet that you may miss it. It may not come in the way you expect either – so be alert for any response.

I always start my contacts with the words, 'Dear God...'   Some Christians say, 'Dear Jesus' or 'Mother Mary' but you could equally effectively say, 'Hello' or 'Hi'. It doesn't matter – in fact very little of the way you commune matters. Once you have 'registered' you don't even need a password – God knows who *you* are and what suits *you* – I'm sure that he is pleased to have you aboard.

Now you will find that things around you *feel* different. If you were lonely before – you won't feel so lonely now. If you felt frustrated with the world before – you will find that your place in it is clearer and you will know what you should be doing. If you felt unloved – you will know that this is no longer the case. If you felt that your life was meaningless – you will soon find what you should be doing to give it meaning. You are now a part of the greatest Being on Earth – God/Mana – and an important part!

Through your eyes, God/Mana will see what is happening where *you* are; through *your* ears he will hear what *you* are hearing and, through *your* mouth, he may even be speaking to whoever *you* are speaking to. If you write, as I do, you may well be writing on his behalf – and that's quite a responsibility. It follows that you must always try and speak or write the truth as you see it and in all your words and acts try and ensure that they fit in with the The Three B's – Be Kind, Be Gentle and Be Fair.

Not only should you now do what is suggested to you (by inspiration or conscience) but you can also ask to be given what you believe you need. In the chapter on Synchronicity, Cosmic Ordering and Prayer we learned that it *is* permitted to ask for material things, especially if having these things helps you serve God/Mana – and that especially includes things that will make you joyful!

Position yourself so that you can experience as much Joy as possible and use it to create as much Love as you can. Look for Joy in as many places as you can. Walk in the countryside, read good books, watch worthwhile films, attend concerts, take part in sport and joint activities with other people. Enjoy the wonderful gift of sharing sexual love. Travel, meet and learn the ways of strangers. Climb mountains, go skinny-dipping in rivers and secluded bays. Be prepared to try different things to what you have been taught – just ensure that what you do is Kind, Gentle and Fair to all concerned. Share this Joy and this Love. Smile at strangers as well as friends and don't be too proud to do menial tasks or to serve other people.

(Sorry! I promised earlier not to preach or tell you what to do, so please just treat the above as worthwhile suggestions.)

Finally, let's suppose for a moment that I have got it all terribly wrong! Maybe the God that I believe in doesn't actually exist, or exists in a different form to that I have proposed. What then? Have we burned our boats, wasted our time, condemned ourselves to everlasting hell? Not at all!

Life will change for you, as it did for me – for the better. If you are living according to the Three Bs (assuming that you weren't before,) your family and friends will notice the difference and be glad of this. As a consequence they will be nicer and more helpful towards you.

All religions that I know of suggest behaviour along the lines of the Three Bs. If decent behaviour is the ticket to their heavenly paradise, following the Three Bs won't disqualify you from entry.

If you exchange a culture of Guilt for a culture of Joy and Love, this can only improve your life.

Part Three. Chapter Eight.

Crossing The River of Disbelief.
An Allegorical Story.

Once upon a time – all the best stories start with 'Once upon a time' – a man and a woman walked sadly along the bank of the *River of Disbelief*. They had heard of a country across the river called *Godlovesyouland* and wanted to cross the river to see if it was as other travellers had described it. As dusk fell, they saw a fire burning on a spit of shingle reaching out into the dark water and walked towards it. Seated near the fire was an elderly man and in the light from his fire they could make out the shape of a small boat pulled up on the shingle.

Seeing them coming, the man rose to his feet, greeted them and invited them to sit by his fire. He offered food and a hot drink, which they gratefully accepted for they had come a long way and had been disappointed many times. The couple had almost given up hope of finding a way to cross this huge river and had even started to believe that *Godlovesyouland* didn't exist. All that had prevented them from turning back was that the wind sometimes blew sweet scents from that direction and once or twice, through the river mists, they had glimpsed tantalising scenes of a gentle land backed by beautiful snow-capped mountains.

They had left the city of *More4me* the day before, to escape the mind-numbing 24/7 muzak and the constant wail of police sirens. In the bleak, friendless countryside of *Grabwhatyoucan* they had spent the night in the travel lodge *'Dawkinsville'* and had asked the proprietor about the best route to *Godlovesyouland*. 'It doesn't exist,' he told them. 'It's just an illusion! Come and I'll show you.'

In the fading light, the travellers had followed him on a well-trodden path up a high hill behind the lodge. It was dark when they reached the top.

'Godlovesyouland?' he said scornfully. 'It's supposed to be over there, but as you can see, it isn't.' He pointed across the river in the darkness. 'See – like I said, it isn't there.'

Despite this, in the morning, they had made their way to the riverbank. Through the dense early morning mists they made out a bridge leading out across the river. This is a fine bridge they were told. 'It was built on ten powerful commandments and established several thousand years ago.'

'Can we cross this fine bridge of yours?' the man asked.

'What race are you?' he was asked and when he replied, he was told that unless their mothers had been born into a different race of people they would not be allowed to use *that* bridge to reach *Godlovesyouland*. The couple turned away and continued down the riverbank.

Soon they saw another bridge with a trickle of people crossing. This looked more hopeful and they asked if they could cross the river by that bridge. 'This is a wonderful bridge,' they were told. 'It was designed by a carpenter's son who lived and died 2000 years ago. He had sketched a simple wooden plank bridge but we didn't like its bare simplicity and we have made it much more glorious. 'Look out there,' the black-robed bridge-keeper said. 'Isn't that wonderful? Look at the fine towers and spires. Look at those amazing domes – look at the richness of it all!'

'What do we have to do to cross this bridge?' the man asked.

'Quite a lot,' he was told and the bridge-keeper described customs and rituals that must be performed, then added. 'And you must first repent of all your sins *and* for the sins of the two people who first lived on Earth.'

'But we never knew these people,' the woman said, 'and I don't recall either of us doing anything we are ashamed of.'

'You must have,' the bridge-keeper replied, 'Or there is nothing for God, through me, to forgive you for. You must feel guilty about *something!*'

'I've had enough of this,' the man said and taking his wife by the hand, walked on down the riverbank. There was still a thick mist hiding the far side of the river.

They came to another bridge, not quite as glorious as the last but still bedecked with towers and spires and were told that it too was based on the simple plank bridge designed 2000 years before. When they asked why it was not the same as the one further upstream they were told that a king had quarrelled with the then chief bridge-keeper five centuries before and had decided to build his own bridge. 'We don't think much of that lot' – The keeper pointed upstream – 'Or any of that lot!' he pointed downstream to where several similar but smaller bridges were showing through the mist.

The man shook his head sadly and said, 'But surely each of the bridges leads to *Godlovesyouland?*

'It isn't like that,' he was told. 'We all know that only *our* bridges are true and safe. Don't trust any of those.'

'Is your bridge open?' the man asked. 'There don't seem to be many people crossing.'

'Well – we're rather busy at the moment with other important things.'

'Such as...? the woman asked.

'Right now, we're trying to decide if women can be bishops. Can you come back in a month or two?'

The couple walked on down the riverbank, passing the smaller bridges, many of which were either boarded up or had been converted into houses and then came to some different ones built in various oriental styles. Huge gongs boomed out from some and on others they could see sacrifices being offered at small shrines and hear the tinkling of bells. No one came and invited them to cross there and they did not understand what was going on or what they might have to do to cross by those bridges.

Then they found another big, strong-looking bridge bedecked with domes and minarets with a sign over the steps leading up to it. The sign read 'PEACE' in a middle-eastern script. The mist was clearing and looking down-stream, the couple could not see any more bridges. 'We'll have to use this one,' the man said. 'It looks like our only chance today. It'll be dark soon.'

'Can we cross the *River of Disbelief* by your fine bridge?' he asked the gate-keeper.

'*You* can,' the man was told. 'But *she* can't come on *this* bridge dressed like that!'

'Come,' said the man turning away sadly. 'We must find somewhere to rest and eat.

'Have you come far?' asked the elderly man on the spit of shingle, reaching for a cooking pan.

'It seems like it,' the man replied, pulling a log towards the fire for his wife to sit on. 'Are there any more bridges downstream?'

'You didn't fancy any of the ones you passed on the way here then?'

'To be truthful – no!'

'It's always good to be truthful – but that stops you crossing many of the bridges. Two eggs each?'

Later, when they were comfortable and well-fed, the woman asked what the man did on that lonely shingle bank.

'I'm a ferryman,' he replied. 'Like you, I didn't find any of the bridges suited me and when I got down here I found a lot of timber washed up on the shingle. My father had been a boatbuilder and I remembered enough to make that little boat.'

'It looks good,' the woman said. 'Where did the wood come from?'

'Now that's a good question and it took me some time to work it out. I think it was thrown away by the bridge-builders upstream. Most of it was simple planks, probably a couple of thousand years old but still sound. Just right for making a small boat.'

The light from the fire was bright enough to show up the boat against the darkness beyond. 'It looks very strong,' said the young man.

'And elegant – if that's the right word?' added the woman. 'Does it have a name?'

Boats are always called *she*', replied the ferryman. 'I call her *The Three Bs.*'

The man and the woman wondered why the boat was called that but were too tired to ask.

'I have a cabin up in the trees,' the ferryman said. 'It's pretty basic but you are welcome to share it if you wish.'

In the morning, the couple were up early but, even so, when they walked down to the shingle bank the ferryman was there, blowing up the embers of the fire to make mugs of coffee for them all.

The young man was examining the boat. 'How much would you charge to row us across the river?' he asked.

'No charge – it's free,' the ferryman replied.

The young man was curious and asked, 'But if you don't charge, why do you do it?'

'I made the boat to take myself across to *Godlovesyouland* because I didn't care for the bridges but, when I got there and found how wonderful it was, I was inspired to row back so that I could offer a ferry service to people like you. We'll go over when you've finished your coffee.'

'Just like that? No pledges, no strange rituals, no payments – nothing like that?'

'Why should there be? *Godlovesyouland* is where everybody is meant to be.'

After rinsing the coffee mugs in the river, the ferryman pushed the boat half off the shingle then helped the travellers aboard, where they sat together on the seat in the stern holding hands. With a well-practised move, the ferryman shoved the bows off the shingle and swung himself on board. He sat on the centre seat facing the travellers, took up the oars and had started to row before the boat reached the main current.

When he was rowing steadily the man said, 'I was going to ask you why this boat is called *The Three B's*.'

The ferryman was silent as he concentrated on rowing around a whirling pool of water formed by rocks beneath the surface. Then he said, 'It's the shorthand for the rules in *Godlovesyouland* – Be kind, Be gentle and Be fair.'

'I like that,' said the woman. 'I really like that!'

'I knew you would,' said the ferryman.

'What other rules are there in *Godlovesyouland*?' the man asked.

'There aren't any,' replied the ferryman. 'Those three cover everything.'

The boat was approaching the riverbank and the ferryman rowed into a quiet place where a backwater carried it alongside a small jetty. The couple climbed out and looked down on the ferryman as he prepared to leave them. 'I must go now, there may be others wanting to cross,' he called up from the boat.

'Before you go, there was something I wanted to know. Are *you* a priest or some kind of holy man?' the woman asked.

'Dear God —No! *I'm* not important. I'm just the ferryman.'

'Thank you for bringing us over, anyway,' the man said. 'Is there something we can do in return?'

'When you've found out how wonderful *Godlovesyouland* is and you want any of your friends or relatives to join you, you could tell them about my ferry service.'

'Will you always be there?'

'I may not be, but the ferry will be. I like to think the little boat I once made will be carrying people like yourselves across this river long after I am gone.' He used an oar to push the boat away from the jetty and out to where the rising sun was drawing up a swirling vapour from the river.

The couple waved as the shape of the boat dissolved into the mist and called out their thanks but all they could hear was the creak of the oars as the ferryman rowed back across the River of Disbelief.

'Come,' said the man, holding out his hand to the woman.

I was going to close this story with the traditional ending, "and they lived happily ever after." But instead of that, I will end it with, "And they lived a life of Joy and Love ever after."

Thank you for staying with me.

Michael Tod.
Abergavenny,
November 2010.

Other books by Michael Tod.

The Silver Tide

The Second Wave

The Golden Flight

All three are now available as a single volume

The Dorset Squirrels

Dolphin Song

God's Elephants

A Curlew's Cry (Poetry)

www.michaeltod.co.uk